FREELANCE WRITING:

DOWN IN THE FOXHOLE WITH PENCIL, NOTEPAD AND CAMERA

FREELANCE WRITING:

DOWN IN THE FOXHOLE WITH PENCIL, NOTEPAD AND CAMERA

Richard T. Edwards

The New
Atlantian Library

The New Atlantian Library
is an imprint of
ABSOLUTELY AMAZING eBOOKS

Published by Whiz Bang LLC, 926 Truman Avenue, Key West, Florida 33040, USA.

For information contact
Publisher@AbsolutelyAmazingEbooks.com

ISBN-13: 0978-1945772870 (New Atlantian Library)
ISBN-10: 1945772875

FREELANCE WRITING:

DOWN IN THE FOXHOLE WITH PENCIL, NOTEPAD AND CAMERA

CONTENTS

HAVE CAMERA, WILL TRAVEL
IT"S YOUR CAREER, NOT MINE
SEXY MEMORIES
HOW TO MAKE YOUR CAR SOUND BAD WHEN IT'S A WHIMP
REVISIONS
FOUR FREELANCE BUSINESS TOOLS YOU CAN'T WORK WITHOUT
1973 WAS A GOOD YEAR FOR ME

FORWARD

What is freelance writing?

Well that depends on what you consider is worthy of your investment of time, experience and equipment, doesn't it?

But if you never went outside your door except to take an occasional image to two, then freelance writing would be a business venture where you offer your services to write, take images, or both to a wide variety of media outlets.

These can include: local small-town newspapers, magazines, television stations; regional and national publications.

The idea here is to tap into an existing cash flow and generate a base of customers you can count on who want to use your services.

Events – what I call Triggers – include flash news, quick news, day in the life of features, regular features, photo-features, human interest articles, news releases, how to articles, editorials and advertorials.

And that's just commercial publications.

Trade publications look for how to articles on selling, marketing, promoting and advertising, and business profiles.

Honestly, if you continue reading, and follow the suggestions, there's no way you're going to fail.

No one likes a wise guy. Unless, of course, you're writing fiction and are planning on using his or her skills for an intended purpose. Comic relief?

"Want to join me at the mile-high club." He asked in a sleazy way. And just about then, the glass broke, and he went flying out the 50th story window.

"Not without a parachute," she said as she turned and walked away. Then looked back, "Smashing, simply smashing."

When you look at a blank sheet of paper, there is no drama, no stories, no people, places and things on it. I am just blank.

But once the words are placed on it and done in a certain way, they can reward you with A's in classes, your work in print, in theater and\or movie rights and awards prizes such as the Pulitzer.

Unfortunately, the fact is, you must start somewhere. Even if you have the natural gift for writing.

The reality is, many can get published, but few survive and even fewer climb to the top of public recognition. I am here to help you get published using the techniques I learned along the way. I have over a 1000 byline in military, consumer and trade publications. And I built them from a lot of trial and error.

This book isn't just all about me and my writing work, it's an example of trial and errors. What one goes through to get published and tips that will help you get published.

Okay, so who am I besides being a published Vietnam Veteran and one who spent 10 years in the Army?

Well, to begin with, I am an X Microsoft employee. Who was what we call in the business of IT a full-time employee (FTE) from 1998 to 2002. Between 1996 to 2013, I have worked for Microsoft in a variety of roles and offering a variety of skill sets.

Before that, I worked at the refineries in and around Lake Charles, LA. I started in 1981 as a helper and left Louisiana as an A Craft outside machinist and B Craft Pipe Fitter. Again, a lot of various jobs in between. Including working with the safety specialist as an assistant and working as a foreman.

I tried going to college at Pima Community College and McNeese State University, but children come first, and the GI Bill didn't cover enough to pay the bills.

I did net 75 credit hours between 1979 and 1989 and majored in English. I wanted to work myself into the MFA program but that never happened. I had some close calls with personnel achievements such as getting published in Arizona Quarterly – they wanted me to rewrite my work to include 1500 words to 3000 words and since I write tight, I found it almost impossible to fluff up the work.

I also know Robert Olen Butler, Shirrel Rhoades and Bruce Helford personally.

In fact, Shirrel Rhoades added two of my photographs to a collection of 135 photographers he considered to have significant impact on the history of photography to the South Carolina Arts and Design (SCAD).

Up until 1996, I added additional income to feed a family of five from my writing and photography. I have thousands of bylines and while I haven't done a body count on how many were commercial and how many were trade publications, a rough guess would be 60%

trades and 40% commercial.

The list of publications is huge. *American Fitness, Better Homes and Gardens, Bicycling Magazine, Bow Hunting Magazine, Army Times, Saga Magazine*, and *Writer* come quickly to mind.

As for the trade publications, these can be broken down into actual business-related publications and actual trade publications.

American Salesman, Small Business Opportunities, Opportunity Magazine, Income Opportunities and *Income Plus* are examples of this kind of publications with my bylines. I was listed as Contributing Editor for *Opportunity Magazine* and have two chapters in a book that *Income Opportunities* published titled *Mind Your Own Business* – edited by Steven Wagner.

I am indirectly responsible for River Boat Gambling in Lake Charles and some of my work in American Salesman has worked its way into an E-Book.

As for pure trade publications, *Army/Navy Surplus, Bicycle Business Journal, Outdoor Power Equipment* and *Unfinished Furniture* are names that come to me quickly.

FICTION AND ART

Believe this or not, one day in April right after my third daughter was born, I sat down and wrote seven 2,100 commercial fiction articles. Between 1980 and 1987, five of those 7 have gone into print. One was revised to exclude a scene where an Army helicopter was used as a vehicle for a bank heist.

We were at the "blues" – meaning into production – stage, when a reality of the fiction took place at Fort Polk.

I also have a bit of a special photo niche that involves body makeup. Like the Goldfinger makeup but different in the later '70s and early '80s to turn heads and attract a cash flow. Nothing pornographic, just art.

The images were stocked by Black Star Publishing in New York and were published worldwide.

The makeup was also on stage with Jefferson Starship.

Currently, I'm working in IT providing consulting services for what is known as Microsoft System Center Suite. When I'm not actually on assignment or working remotely from home, I work on my blogs, stay up on the never-ending changes in what I support and create software that I hope will increase income revenues.

IN THE BEGINNING THERE WAS A BLANK SHEET OF PAPER

Imagine, for a moment that you were in Vietnam, you have 90 days left In Country and you were just given an assignment as the Battalion stringer. You don't know an F-stop from shutter speed, and you certainly don't know how to write for the military much less what it takes to write a feature about your unit.

What you do know is the place you've been calling home for the past 270 days has a division level public affairs office and some of the men you met there were going gaga over the images you took with your Ashi Pentax. There is also a recreational services photo lab available to you as well.

Where would you start?

Well, I know where I started. I focused on what the Battalion Commander wanted me to do and that was take images of awards and decorations. And that also led to some quick publication visibility for our battalion in the form of a picture and a cutline. A cutline is nothing more than a quick who, what when and where sentence of information taped to the back of an image.

But an event happened a few weeks prior that played on my mind as being newsworthy. And I wanted to title it, "So why are you whispering."

Prior to my assignment to the Battalion

Headquarters, I was saying goodbye to my friends at A Company 5th Transportation Battalion as they were very instrumental in helping me from a logistical effort on rebuilding our unit.

I carried a CEOI and had my jeep radio on while I was talking to my friends at A Company when I heard some chatter between one of our pilots and some ARVN ground troops. Of course, I couldn't hear the ground troops, but I could hear our pilot talking to them. Went something like this.

"Roger, confirming what your telling me that you estimate a force of at least 128 enemy soldiers in round straw topped buildings. Please confirm your identity."

"Roger, passing over your credentials for confirmation.

"Why are you whispering?"

"Roger, is this better?"

You can bet that in less that 3 minutes me and my jeep were back over to our helicopter pad known as the bull pen and I was helping to load up the AH-1G Cobras with 17 and 10-pound rockets.

By the time it was all over, we had a confirmed kill count of 128 NVA soldiers with 0 friendly casualties on the ground or in the air.

The problem was, when you're that close to the action, it is hard to take images of what was going happening on the flight line. Although a good friend of mine who I knew as LT Craig Gies had taken images of the event, I wasn't aware they had existed until recently.

On top of all of that, B Battery was not the only Battery from the 4th Battalion, 77th Field Artillery that was involved with the incident. So, I went with:

4th Battalion, 77th Field Artillery (ARA) Kills 128 NVA In One Day

Camp Eagle, July 21, 1970

The 4th Battalion, 77th Field Artillery (ARA) Kills 128 NVA In One Day near Firebase Ripcord. The confirmed kills were confirmed by ARVN soldiers who called in support when they spotted on of the Battalions' Cobra passing through the area heading for refueling and rearming.

The air-based conversation between the pilot and the friendly ground forces went something like this:

"Roger, confirming what your telling me that you estimate a force of at least 128 enemy soldiers in round straw topped buildings. Please confirm your identity."

"Roger, passing over your credentials for confirmation.

"Why are you whispering?"

"Roger, is this better?"

The Two-minute sections, consisting of two AH-1G Cobras, from A Battery, B Battery and C Battery of the 4th Battalion, 77th Field Artillery (ARA), 101st Airborne Division (Air

Mobile) sprung into action and additional resources were prepared to engage in the action if necessary.

There were 0 causalities of friendly ground forces or from the 4th Battalion, 77th Field Artillery (ARA) and was recorded as the largest single day NVA KIA's so far by the 4th Battalion, 77th Field Artillery (ARA), 101st Airborne Division (Air Mobile).

That was the extent of the news release. And had I not written it, only those involved in the event would have ever known about it.

Of course, I had wished I could do more. But learning how to write and acquiring news event driven articles got slow after Firebase Ripcord few and far between. I did do a story on an orphanage up near Hue and took images in the front seat of a Cobra showing rockets in front of the Cobra during SERTS training at Camp Evans that were used in a magazine called *Rendezvous with Destiny* but that was basically it.

I went home reading in *Army Times* on the Freedom Plane, my story I had written about the orphanage. And at that point, I realized, maybe, just maybe, this was something I wanted to do for a living.

RE-LIVING CHILDHOOD DAYS

Your writing shouldn't be just about writing someone else's story. It should be about you was well. No one says you must get everything you write published. Below reflect those two statements.

ON AN ADVENTURE

At the Memorial Field. On the northwest corner of the track was a small swamp, where memories of cattails, dragonflies, frogs, salamanders and lightning bugs keeping me busy during those long summer evenings were created.

A lot of pretending went into those childhood days. I was out in the middle of the jungle fighting mosquitoes the size of dragoon flies, in a different part of the world, each turn along the path another adventure in its own.

Okay, honestly, the real danger was me getting my shoes wet, muddy or both and then getting whipping for that once my mother found out and my father got home.

Right now, I am following the riverbed stalking the elusive and poisonous salamander.

The way you would catch one of these creatures I would begin my mental diary of my daily travels along the riverbed – a spring fed waterway of 3 inches – was to overturn the larger rocks above the giant waterfall –

the height of a pencil – and allow the otherwise crystal clear water to muddy up a bit and hide the salamander within until it came upon another giant rock – the size of a silver dollar downstream.

This one was a rather remarkable color and size. Almost a bright orange, its little body and four legs desperately looking for cover and hoping its little tail would stick out too far out from under the rock as to be seen by a sharp-eyed bird of prey flying high above the scene below.

Which would have probably been one of the ducks that lived in the swampy spring fed area just north west of track where cattails were the cities of the swamp and the sweet smell of honey suckle made the area smell like sweet sawdust.

But there were other creatures that lurked in my own private world of mystery and adventure. Fogs, crickets and tadpoles pelted the airways with their distinctive mating calls.

To say they were elusive was an understatement! Get too close to their territory and the theater of life shut down like a switch. As though someone just turned on the sounds of nature. Waiting for you to break a twig and, when you did, seemed like twenty frogs plopping into the shallow water in short order.

The biggest plop you heard was the biggest fog in the swamp and that was where you wanted to sit and wait. The larger, older ones who survived our human hunts learned to come up to the top slowly under the protection of the lilies, get some fresh air and dive back down under the cover of the murky water.

This was a game of patience and the winner takes

all. You moved your fine woven fishing net with long wooden handle over where you spotted the frog and quickly drove the net down upon the frog twisting the net around the frog and back up into the air.

After a couple dozen times of trial and error, you finally get the timing and the technique down to a science and the frog was yours.

It was the thrill of catching a frog that made it fun. Only time I didn't let the frog go was when a high school kid asked me if he could have the one I just caught.

Other than that, it was just fun for me to see life ebb and flow in the swamp. And as I grew older, the dragonflies and lightning bugs just painted more memories of those days when life was as simple as Mother Nature.

WRITE AN ARTICLE I WILL ENJOY

When you don't know me, what makes you think you can write an article I will enjoy?

The answer to this question may be worth millions. Amazing how so many writers never do get it.

Every reader shares a common human trait: curiosity.

Think of the beginning of your work to tap into that curiosity as a reader and become their eyes and ears as a method to satisfy their need to know. And accomplished the way they read.

So, I get out of the Army in 1979 to pursue a degree. I was already a published U.S Army writer and photography with over 250 articles published and close to 1000 images.

To put it bluntly, I was spoiled rotten. And I would, eventually, learn to be my own worst enemy and must edit my work.

Back then, too, in the ancient history days of no grammar or spell checkers, this was a nightmare for a dyslexic who spelled also aslo.

Anyway, as it turned out, my wife was pregnant with my 3rd child and I needed to go from Pima College in Tucson, AZ, to McNeese State University in Lake Charles, LA.

When I started at McNeese I heard about an MFA in creating writing and so, I wanted to find out more about the two very special friends: Leo Marcello and Ronald Johnson. Leo – who as passed away – was the prof for Poetry and Ron was the Prof for fiction.

Both were brilliant in their own specialties some interesting acquaintances.

Well, as you can pretty much imagine, the years passed and so did the opportunities to go to school. And my snowballs chance in hell start in the world of commercial and trade publications blossomed to the steady monthly bylines, 3 cover images and a contributing editor role for Opportunity Magazine.

I did take one fiction class with Ron. Which, as always proves to be embarrassing as my high school teacher did the same. Why do they always rant and rave about my fiction and non-fiction.

Anyway, Ron compared me to Joyce Carol Oates. Who the hell is she, right?

Listen to me. If you're good, there is something about the way you play with words without even thinking about it that can really freak you out when you hear those same lines being read by someone else.

And they sound even better!

So, work at the plants, wanting to get back into the saddle, when Ron left and was replaced by Robert Olen Butler, I would call him to see if I wasn't dealing with the good cop\bad cop line of succession.

The red light was in play and I put icy headset back on its cradle now starting to thaw out.

I'm indirectly responsible for Riverboat Gambling in Lake Charles, LA. Opportunity Magazine – own by Shirrel Rhoades at the time – let me have the entire publication to focus on how small businesses survived the 1980's Oil bust.

One of the articles was on the Downtowner Hotel and described its location. Apparently, Marv Griffin and Players International thought it was an ideal location for a Riverboat Casino.

I also took a lot of trips back and for from Lake Charles, La to Tucson, AZ

I won't go into why but will just say that there was a sign on the door on the door where books on how to write were located that said Arizona Quarterly.

So, I knocked on the door, was greeted by an elderly lady who handed me their writers guide and a copy of the publication.

I wrote a fiction piece and sent it to them. I write tight. So, when you're told write 1,500 more words into a 3,000-word article that *Arizona Quarterly* tells you they need. I didn't know what to do.

So, once again, I'm back in Tucson, in the U\A library and knocking on the door.

I really felt bad I had let them down. An older gentleman introduced himself to me as the editor and told me to come with him. He pulled out an issue and told me to close my eyes. Hiding the authors name he asked me to read it. Summary, it was about a janitor who would throw down his large cigars and leave them there in the female teacher's bathroom. And the new female principle threatened to fire him

End of story, she did. Closing with the scene of her going to the female teacher's bathroom with one in every toilet. (Okay, there might have been a pile of them in each; I don't remember.)

That's the best I can remember of it.

So, he asked, “What do you think?”

I started shaking my head, “Mine’s better.”

The editor nodded his head in agreement. “Yes, but yours could use some polishing up. And that’s not the point. The point is, I saw potential in the both of you. Which is why I am publishing her work.”

As he rolled his finger off the author’s name, it said, “Joyce Carol Oates.”

The point to all of this is: You never know what effect you have, how your work can change lives unless you work your craft, rewrite and rewrite your work so that it gets published and you grow up with a legacy.

HOW DO I COME UP WITH IDEAS THAT SELL?

Which is not a good question to ask me.

Why?

Because I would ask fiction or non-fiction?

Then you would say non-fiction.

Then I would have to ask you: For what, trade or commercial publication?

Then you would say commercial.

Then I would ask what kind group category?

And at this point you would walk away.

Why?

Because you don't think this way.

An organized mind can write anything and for any publication if the information is organized to suit the needs for acceptance.

Suiting the needs for acceptance is the place where the question gets raised: How do I come up with ideas that sell?

There are some very hard stop decisions an editor goes through to determine if the article is for his\her publication. Many of these are universal. Meaning, you don't have to read the guidelines to know these are expected of you as a writer. These are:

The article needs to finish at the acceptable length.

The article needs to be double-spaced.

The article needs to be clean of spelling and grammatical errors.

Then comes the specific details that earns you acceptance:

The article needs a subject that the publication wants to publish.

The article needs to be about something that the readers will want to experience.

The title of the article needs to draw the reader into the body of the article.

The body of the work moves the reader through the important points that support the title.

The end of the article summing up all the points presented into a tidy conclusion.

The last stack of articles – the ones which will either get accepted or have a personal rejection – involves the following:

Does the article hook the reader into wanting to read past the first sentence?

Does the article also address why the reader should know these things?

Are the facts correct?

Are the statements accurate?

Does the body of the work invoke more questions than it answers?

JUST THE FACTS, MA'AM

There was a TV show back in my day called *Dragnet*. Supposedly, Detective Sergeant Joseph "Joe" Friday had said this. Apparently, he didn't. In fact, Friday never actually said this in an episode, but it was featured in Stan Freberg's works parodying Dragnet. How's that for checking facts?

Anyway, the point to be made here is, when you first get started on the road to becoming a published writer, the first thing you should be asking is, well, what makes a news story a news story?

After all, there should be a basic and standard tried and true way to generate quick copy. A way you should say what it needs to say and be done with it, right?

A good reporter needs to collect the facts and then collect any events which occurred before or after the incident. The 6 W's.

The core elements of a new article are the following:

- Who
- What
- When
- Where
- Why
- How

First thing I must admit I really want to have fun

with this but for the sake of professionalism, we'll do this by the book.

Who: Frank Marks, age 21, single and owns a kitten.

What: Broke his arm

When: Yesterday, November 16, 2018

Where: Near his home

Why: Trying the get his kitten down from a tree

When: It got scared by a mean bulldog from next door

How: Grabbing the kitten, he lost his footing and fell 7 feet

Headline:

MAN BREAKS ARM TRYING TO GET HIS KITTEN OUT OF TREE

This is what is known as a Who lead:

> Frank Marks, age 21 who resides at 224 Brookshire St. broke his arm while trying to grab his kitten from a 12-foot tree in front of his house after the neighbors' pet bull dog jumped the fence and scared the little feline to the very top.
>
> Both survived the ordeal.

This is what is known as a What lead:

> A broken arm is the result of Yesterday's calamity when Frank Marks, age 21, who lives at 224 Brookshire St, when he tried rescue his kitten from a 12-foot tree in front of his house after the neighbors' pet

bull dog jumped the fence and scared the little feline to the very top.

Both survived the ordeal.

This is what is known as a When lead:

Yesterday, November 16, 2018, Frank Marks broke his arm while trying to grab his kitten from a 12-foot tree in front of his house after the neighbors' pet bull dog jumped the fence and scared the little feline to the very top.

Both survived the ordeal.

This is what is known as a Where lead:

224 Brookshire St. was the scene of a minor accident when Frank Marks, age 21 tried rescue his kitten from a 12-foot tree in front of his house after the neighbors' pet bull dog jumped the fence and scared the little feline to the very top.

Both survived the ordeal.

This is what is known as a Why lead:

After the neighbors' pet bulldog jumped the fence and scared kitten up a 12-foot tree in front of Frank Marks house at 224 Brookshire St. Marks lost his footing grabbing the feline and the two fell to the ground. Approximately 7 feet.

Both survived the ordeal.

Once you've gotten the story to this point, you can have a ball with it. This type of story has all kinds of possibilities. Descriptive quotes Marks, the owners of the pit bull, the police, and the fire department.

The key is theme or slant. And you get to play god. Here are some ideas:

- Call the fire department they are the pros
- The neighbors need to secure their dog better
- The neighborhood comes through and helps Mark with the cat until his arm healed.

So, what is this kind of article called?

Reverse Pyramid and if you do extend it out beyond the who, what, when, where, why and how, keep the supporting paragraphs short, with the most important facts about what happened before during and after the incident first.

WILL THE REAL CHRIS POWEL PLEASE STAND DOWN?

Anyone remember a guy by the name of Chris Powel?

No?

He's the one with the show called: *Extreme Makeover*.

Still, no?

Believe me, you aren't alone.

Well, whether you do or not, the fact is, you just got a taste of inquisitive writing.

THE DRIVING FORCE OF POPULARITY ON THE INTERNET.

You have a book and you want it published, see if the book author has an associates page and what he or she is willing to pay you to promote the work.

The first involves stagnation in aggressive and creative diversity on the Internet. People have simply nothing better to choose from and feel comfortable going to Facebook, and the rest of the monopolized information resources.

The second, people are using cell phones and icon-based applications are used. So, instead of having to search, all the user must do is tap the screen and they are instantly transported to their favorite social gatherings.

The third is legalizing a 25-year attack on freedom of speech and expression on the Internet. The powers to be have been doing a good job of putting that in place since 2012 and just needed the law changed to make their illegal practices legal.

Again, this is all speculative and sidestepping why you can tap into it using inquisitive writing.

Here's how it works: You create a blog and have a page about how you love watches and clocks. Every time you mention a brand and provide a link, you get credit for the referral.

Your links are based on an association with the company mentioned and, should that product sell, you are paid a commission for the sale.

IT'S A MATTER OF VISIBILITY AND PERSUASION

Should I have a blog or a website or both?

If there is one thing I've learned after interviewing small business owners throughout the United States is that potential and loyal customers are having one thing in common: They want to hear the name of your business and the bond between it, them and the products and\or services you have earned their business with.

It is what is known as Branding. Done correctly, it combines marketing, promoting and advertising in a single package.

Yes, I know that market, promotions and advertising are normally thought of as three different skills you need to develop if you're going to make writing and\or photography a business and turn a profit.

Sadly, few consider awareness as being just as important if not the most important factor in the success of a gaining a loyal customer base.

If Shirrel Rhoades is reading this one, he's already smiling for two reasons. One, he has heard all of this before from me and two he also knows where I'm about to go with this. And here we go.

There is nothing more important for your small

business venture than to realize you must first become an effect listener.

Can a blog do that? No. Can a website do that? No. You are the one that needs to go to potential customers or at the very least have an associates program.

When disappointments are turned into a positive experience for your potential customers by the way you define their issues and resolve them, your potential customer becomes a local customer because he or she realizes you did listen.

The only way you can be an effective listener is by listening and putting yourself in their shoes and appreciate their concerns and disappointments.

Remember, too. Objections are nothing more than an unanswered solution to a problem that needs to be resolved to land a contract with the client.

A DAY IN THE LIFE OF AN ARTICLE

I may not have mentioned this already but Faction – which uses drama to set the stage – is a technique you use when you want to pull the reader into the otherwise boring non-fiction story.

What I didn't mention is that Faction, is also a way to write chapters for novels. *Harry Potter* an example.

Okay, let's switch to a rather quick example of A Day in the Life of an Article.

Like the Faction format, you first need to collect the facts about the person, place or thing your wanting to reveal to others as you go along.

But unlike Faction, the goal here is to have the reader see through the eyes of the person who is the person or who works with the place or thing the article is about.

The questions you need to ask are:

- Who opens the store?
- What are the tasks need to be done before the store opens?
- Which ones must be done and why?
- What happens if that person is sick?
- After your store is open, what are the busiest times for your store?
- Are your store sales based on seasonal sales?
- Who restocks your shelves and how often are

they turned?

- What sells the most, products or services?
- How many employees do you have?
- What incentive programs do you have to maintain your staff?
- What incentive programs do you have for your customers?
- Describe how your business operates.
- Who closes the store?

For example.

Its 7 a.m., already the pets in the store are up and wanting to get fed after all, they need food to put up with the humans who will take them home and take care of them.

Even the king snake wants to curl itself around its next meal.

For Tim Johnson, at Pets Are Us, all of them depend on him to be there in the morning, to clean up the mess in the cages, make the place smell nice for the customers and do the rests of the tasks the assistant manager does to keep the pet store running as smooth as glass.

Then comes the quotes from him about what he must do to prepare the story for the business day and as we are walked through each section how each section is operated and maintained by the store's employees.

The story, of course, ends with a descriptive lockup and a reflection from Tim Johnson as he heads for his car.

LIAR, LIAR, PANTS ON FIRE

A fact is a lie until it is proven 100% true.

There is a sucker born every day. Never become one.

News is not news if it is located at the grocery checkout.

If a story plays on emotions, it better be fantasy or a man with a Bible in his hand. Which may possibly be one in the same.

(I still want Santa Claus to come down the chimney and eat my peanut butter fudge).

For every action, there is an equal and opposite reaction. As a writer, you must figure out how what writing has no equal and opposite reaction on your existence.

When someone comes in with a story directing it towards a bleeding-heart person, you might want to find out if that someone isn't motivated to gain the most from its visibility.

Enter my world of true lies. The story I'm about to use here as an example of all the above writing ethics and pitfalls is one that I personally find disturbing on so many levels for so many different reasons. To say it hit a nerve is a gross understatement.

But before I go into the story and the reasons why it is bad – not only for the "hero," veterans and, more importantly, homeless Veterans – I want to admit to a couple of things.

There's no real Christmas tree, no presents under it for me to share with my wife, no presents to share with our children because we can't afford such things and should the car we're driving break down – which it is threatening to do – we have no transportation.

In other words, we're one step on a banana peel away from being on the streets ourselves.

So, yeah, when I hear about a homeless veteran man who looks drugged out of his mind is seen as a hero and the story goes viral, I instinctively look for the real reason why this all got started in the first place.

Wasn't hard to find. A pickle jar with a brand name the same as the damsel in distress's name. And I'm betting her, and her boyfriend will be running around in their limo because they used a media system vulnerable to credibility issues and combined it with a PBS documentary on the Vietnam War and the months when people want to give money to the poor and the homeless.

By the way the media does consider retractions to be a sure kiss of death.

The magnitude equal to the fate of the two who sold the com to the emperor who believed nudity was a new clothing line and the Music Man who was about to get tarred and feathered using a similar con.

So, when someone says, "Homeless man gives woman his last 20 for gas at a gas station and that turns out to be a lie, wouldn't you expect the story to be retracted, GoFundMe to shut off the cash flow and that would be the end of the story, right?

Wrong. The press couldn't back out of the story.

Another headline said he gave her his last 20 because she ran out of gas.

Well, if he gives her his last 20 and the car is not at a gas station what the heck good is it to give her a 20 in the first place?

Obviously, that didn't happen either.

In fact, according to the latest story, he did take a red gas container and used his last 20 (even that is suspect) on gas.

Try $5 worth of gas.

Plenty enough money to go to McDonalds, have a big breakfast and a refillable cup of coffee. After that, he will be on the corner with his sign panhandling for the next day's food and money for his drug habit.

Which by the way was never talked about until $360,000 was generated by this well-crafted con.

The veteran, by the way wrote on his Facebook page about a similar situation that occurred in 2012 where he offered to help a lady who ran out of gas in an intersection and had a flat tire.

And that story – if true – didn't make front-page news.

Come to think of it, when I saved a little boy's life in Louisiana because he would have bled to death, that didn't make the newspapers either. My daughter, Mary Edwards, remembers it.

It was good enough for me to know I did save a life that day.

To conclude, without the press, there would be no heroes.

The question here is how would the press react to a bum off the streets telling this story verses the business lady who said the same story?

And I know what the answer would be: A snowballs chance in hell.

THE FEATURE ARTICLE

What is a feature article? I know his is going to sound ridiculously trite but whatever the editorial limits and reader thinks it should be.

Once you gather the facts, all the paragraphs you want to use to make the story come alive for the reader must be harmonized into a single purpose and that then becomes the subject and title for the feature.

Here's an example of how I go through the process.

First, I have a purpose. I want to make a clear distinction between A and B. Doesn't matter what it is, to make that distinction happen, I must understand why that is a point to be made. If clothes make the man, facts make or break the feature writer.

For example, look at this and compare it to the one below it:

What I'm about to tell you will change the way you see a Cobra helicopters forever.

By all rights the Cobra helicopter was in a league of its own and stripped of any weapons systems, they all looked the same and had all the characteristics of speed, sleek design and responsiveness.

It was the way – the configuration – in which the armament systems were added to the turret and the wing stores that made them different. That was predicated by the missions of the units using them. That was where the line drawn in the sand. That was the difference between a Cavalry Cobra – known as a gunship and the Aerial Rocket Artillery Cobra – known an Aerial Artillery firing platform.

The latter made famous by the press, the former, going through the various development steps leading up to the Apache helicopter and its role as an amour and tank killer.

Here's the other:

In Vietnam, the sleek looking AH-1G Cobra had two distinct missions: A Gunship or an aerial rocket artillery platform. Unfortunately, the press was unable to make that decision and thought all AH-1G Cobras where Gunships. The other went on to pave way for the Apache helicopter.

Which one would you use?

In 1980, I wrote:

In Vietnam, the Cobra pilots had a saying "Killing in our business and business is good." Today that saying has been changed. "Tank killing is our business and, someday, business will be good."

Kind of prophetic since I made the second one up myself. And Desert Storm proved me right.

Anyway, while I'm about Cobra helicopters, I want to pull in a feature article here that I helped to write and was my first big photo-feature. The above were examples of how some of what I wrote back then has matured over time and my writing has become much clearer.

I look back at this first article and realized just how blessed I was to have others work on the piece beside myself. So, let me start off by saying, the slant of this article was to show the readers the difference between Aerial Rocket Artillery – ARA– and gunships.

It's 2200 hours. You're on guard duty, it's raining, and you're cold and wet.

Suddenly, the skylights up and there are flashes everywhere. Then, after a pause, there is a frightening roar. But other than being afraid and despite the weather conditions, the whole scene makes you feel and you watch with fascination knowing that an AH-1G Cobra helicopter is pouring its awesome fire power on a suspected enemy position.

The next day you are driving around Camp Eagle and you see some Cobras sitting on a helipad. You grab your camera, walk up and stand beside one of them while your buddy snaps a picture. When the prints come back, you show your friends, "Here I am standing next to an ARA Cobra."

First, I didn't write this. But it worked for the time. Not anymore. Here is the story the way I would write it today.

> **Today was your day to perform perimeter guard duty. With the rest of the men this leaky poncho night you're about to have your usual Officer in Charge, Of the Guard pep talk about not getting caught sleeping, don't play hero, smoke light yourself as a target. In other words, the usual grind of things to do and not to do.**
>
> **You could tape record the entire speech and each OIC OG would be the same.**

Except for tonight.

"Got a special treat for you men tonight. The ARA Cobra pilots want to hone their skills doing night time..."

Seems like everyone around you just got hit with a shot of excitement including yourself. Behind the safety of the line of perimeter guard positions and inside the safety of Camp Eagle, it's seldom that you get a front seat view of Cobras working a target during the day, much less at night.

You focus back on what the OIC OG is saying, "This will happen at 2400 hours. Yes, I know this will cut into your mad minute. No leg popping flares and emptying a clip on a monkey. Let's let the pilots and the Cobras do work for a living.

"Hey," whispers your buddy, "What is ARA?"

You shrug your shoulders.

"And in anyone is wondering, the ARA stands for Aerial Rocket Artillery."

"Aerial cannon cockers. Why does that not sound normal to me? What do they do have flying leprechauns controlling the rockets?"

Impossible to maintain a modicum of seriousness, you break

out in a fit of laughter.

"Is there a problem, soldier?"

"No, sir, he," point behind you, said, "asked, what do they do have flying leprechauns controlling the rockets?"

Even the Officer of the Guard was laughing and then everyone calmed down.

"Sir, what does that Aerial Rocket Artillery do that the Gunships from the Cavalry do?"

Officer of the Guard thought about it for a moment and then said, "The ARA brings to the infantry fighting on the ground two Cobras with 144 2.75-inch rockets, a few thousand rounds of mini gun ammo and around 500 40mm grenades. The Cavalry Gunships on the other hand wait for the OH-6 helicopter to drop smoke and then obliterates the area with their 30mm canons, mini guns and 40mm grenades.

"Any more questions?"

Someone had to ask, "Sir, are you supplying popcorn and soda pop?"

"Party's over men. Time to go to work. Excused."

"Hey," pokes your buddy, "How quick can you grab your camera? Make sure you have film in it this

time!"

This was promising to be one special night.

----

transition:

The 101st Airborne Division Airmobile is one of two airmobile divisions had an Aerial Rocket Artillery Battalion assigned to it. It had the 4th Battalion, 77th Aerial Field Artillery.

The other, 2nd Battalion, 20th Artillery was assigned to the 1st Cavalry Division along with F Battery, 79th Artillery.

Each ARA battalion had 36 AH-1G Cobras. Each Battery having 12 of the 36.

A Battery – called the Dragons – with red arrows painted on the Cobra's tail booms was in Phu Bai, B Battery – called the El Toros – with their white arrows painted on their Cobra's tail booms was located at Camp Eagle. And C Battery – called the Griffins – with their blue arrows painted on their Cobra's tail booms were located at Camp Evans.

Back to The Story:

2400 hours arrive. You've got your camera on your tripod. Crickets are the only sound churning up the midnight air. High above you the presence of Huey can be heard faintly and over the distance of less than a quarter mile, someone is heard yelling, "Fire Mission."

Seconds later, the engines and the whoosh, whoosh sounds of rotor blades increasing in speed can be heard. A minute later, you hear them take off and then there's silence.

----

transition:

The Cobras that they heard take off belong to B Battery and are part of what is known as a section. The Battery is divided into groups called sections 2-minute, 5 minutes, 15 minute and standby. The idea is that within the designated time, two Cobras would launch within the designated time.

When a section is launched, each moves up. So, the 5-minute section becomes that 2-minute section.

Artillery Aviators and Warrant Officers perform the tasks of flying and gunnery positions and once in the air are given encrypted grid

coordinates which they decipher in the air using a CEOI to the location where friendly ground forces need up close and personal Artillery Support.

Back to The Story:

Suddenly, the sky lights up with the flare ship dropping flares.

"You ready to see some serious heavy-duty stuff," shouted your buddy.

The first Cobra can be seen starting a dive from 3000 feet and sends two rockets hurdling toward the ground at 6,700 miles per hour. The white phosphorous can be seen marking the target and as the first Cobra begins its climb back up to 3000 feet, the other Cobra begins its dive a steady stream of tracers is seen and focused from the two still smoking white phosphorous rounds.

----

transition:

Unlike the Cavalry Cobra gunship, on ARA Cobra can carry a total of 72 rockets, and have a turret configuration of two mini guns, or twin 40mm grenade launchers or one

of each.

The mini gun can fire 3,000 rounds per minute and have a red tipped tracer round for every 5 rounds fired. That solid looking line of bullets is one of 5 and the gun itself capable of hitting every square inch of a football field.

Back to The Story:

Now, the second Cobra starts its run and sends four more rockets hurdling toward the ground these sounds more powerful and are as lethal as they sound. In close quarters, the have a kill range of 5 meters. Some can penetrate double and triple canopy before hitting the ground. With lethal force.

Climbing back up to 3000 feet the second cobra gets out of the way of the first and nothing, but solid rockets come flying from its wing stores. A total of 18 pairs.

----

transition:

Because the pilot and the gunner can see what is going on below then, they are able to access the situation and decide if additional resources are

needed as well as decide if the resources should be additional AH-1G ARA Cobras or something with a bit more punch. Like an F-4 Phantom.

Back to The Story:

The cycle of diving from 3000 feet to 1500 feet continues for the next 7 minutes and then, the only thing left is the smell of exploded ordinance drifting towards your position from ground zero. Where there are now potholes where plant life and small animals called home.

After an exciting night, you get picked up and dropped off near your hooch. Thinking about eating breakfast, you secure your TA-50 gear, lock up your camera and head to the mess hall.

---

transition:

Aside from what the soldiers saw that night, the ARA performs other duties such as preparing an LZ for the arrival of ground troops and protecting them while being dropped off, supporting Command and Control North activities, escorting Air Force

defoliant missions and protecting VIPs such as Bob Hope and USO Shows.

Back to The Story:

Fellow soldiers you were with on guard duty appear all excited, talking faster than usual and using their hands like Cobras in the sky laying down rockets and spitting out lead through their fingers.

"Hell, of a night, buddy."

"Yeah," you say, "With that type of action going on every night, you would want to do guard duty every night."

"Heard there's a cure for that kind of thinking. It's over at the corner of What Are You Insane and Psych Ward Avenue."

That put a smile on your face while pouring some coffee into the white ceramic mug.

"Listen, I've still got a couple of shots left on the roll in the camera, why don't we take the jeep and drop by where those Cobra took off and landed. It's on our way to the PX. I can take one of you and you one of me and then I'll order two sets of prints. One for me and one for you."

"You'd do that?"

"Sure. You're the one with the jeep."

"Deal."

Not the best but better than the original.

With that said, let's get out of the focus on feature writing and focus on how marketing articles have changed dramatically from my time in the past and the way it is done currently.

If I had a good idea for an article and I thought it would be a good fit for a publication, I simply wrote it, submitted it and moved to the next article I wanted to write.

Of course, it didn't start out this way. I did what everyone else did. Write introduction and sent a self-addressed stamped envelope so the publication could then reject my introduction.

Now, here's the same thing without the editorial notations:

Today was your day to perform perimeter guard duty. With the rest of the men this leaky poncho night you're about to have your usual Officer in Charge, Of the Guard pep talk about not getting caught

sleeping, don't play hero, smoke light yourself as a target. In other words, the usual grind of things to do and not to do.

You could tape record the entire speech and each OIC OG would be the same.

Except for tonight.

"Got a special treat for you men tonight. The ARA Cobra pilots want to hone their skills doing night time..."

Seems like everyone around you just got hit with a shot of excitement including yourself. Behind the safety of the line of perimeter guard positions and inside the safety of Camp Eagle, it's seldom that you get a front seat view of Cobras working a target during the day, much less at night.

You focus back on what the OIC OG is saying, "This will happen at 2400 hours. Yes, I know this will cut into your mad minute. No leg popping flares and emptying a clip on a monkey. Let's let the pilots and the Cobras do work for a living.

"Hey," whispers your buddy, "What is ARA?"

You shrug your shoulders.

"And in anyone is wondering, the ARA stands for Aerial Rocket

Artillery."

"Aerial cannon cockers. Why does that not sound normal to me? What do they do have flying leprechauns controlling the rockets?"

Impossible to maintain a modicum of seriousness, you break out in a fit of laughter.

"Is there a problem, soldier?"

"No, sir, he," point behind you, said, "asked, what do they do have flying leprechauns controlling the rockets?"

Even the Officer of the Guard was laughing and then everyone calmed down.

"Sir, what does that Aerial Rocket Artillery do that the Gunships from the Cavalry do?"

Officer of the Guard thought about it for a moment and then said, "The ARA brings to the infantry fighting on the ground two Cobras with 144 2.75-inch rockets, a few thousand rounds of mini gun ammo and around 500 40mm grenades. The Cavalry Gunships on the other hand wait for the OH-6 helicopter to drop smoke and then obliterates the area with their 30mm canons, mini guns and 40mm grenades.

"Any more questions?"

Someone had to ask, "Sir, are you supplying popcorn and soda pop?"

"Party's over men. Time to go to work. Excused."

"Hey," pokes your buddy, "How quick can you grab your camera? Make sure you have film in it this time!"

This was promising to be one special night.

The 101st Airborne Division Airmobile is one of two airmobile divisions had an Aerial Rocket Artillery Battalion assigned to it. It had the 4th Battalion, 77th Aerial Field Artillery.

The other, 2nd Battalion, 20th Artillery was assigned to the 1st Cavalry Division along with F Battery, 79th Artillery.

Each ARA battalion had 36 AH-1G Cobras. Each Battery having 12 of the 36.

A Battery – called the Dragons – with red arrows painted on the Cobra's tail booms was in Phu Bai, B Battery – called the El Toros – with their white arrows painted on their Cobra's tail booms was located at Camp Eagle. And C Battery – called the Griffins – with their blue arrows painted on their Cobra's tail booms

were located at Camp Evans.

2400 hours arrive. You've got your camera on your tripod. Crickets are the only sound churning up the midnight air. High above you the presence of Huey can be heard faintly and over the distance of less than a quarter mile, someone is heard yelling, "Fire Mission."

Seconds later, the engines and the whoosh, whoosh sounds of rotor blades increasing in speed can be heard. A minute later, you hear them take off and then there's silence.

The Cobras that they heard take off belong to B Battery and are part of what is known as a section. The Battery is divided into groups called sections 2-minute, 5 minutes, 15 minute and standby. The idea is that within the designated time, two Cobras would launch within the designated time.

When a section is launched, each moves up. So, the 5-minute section becomes that 2-minute section.

Artillery Aviators and Warrant Officers perform the tasks of flying and gunnery positions and once in the air are given encrypted grid coordinates which they decipher in the air using a CEOI to the location

where friendly ground forces need up close and personal Artillery Support.

Suddenly, the sky lights up with the flare ship dropping flares.

"You ready to see some serious heavy-duty stuff," shouted your buddy.

The first Cobra can be seen starting a dive from 3000 feet and sends two rockets hurdling toward the ground at 6,700 miles per hour. The white phosphorous can be seen marking the target and as the first Cobra begins its climb back up to 3000 feet, the other Cobra begins its dive a steady stream of tracers is seen and focused from the two still smoking white phosphorous rounds.

Unlike the Cavalry Cobra gunship, on ARA Cobra can carry a total of 72 rockets, and have a turret configuration of two mini guns, or twin 40mm grenade launchers or one of each.

The mini gun can fire 3,000 rounds per minute and have a red tipped tracer round for every 5 rounds fired. That solid looking line of bullets is one of 5 and the gun itself capable of hitting every square inch of a football field.

Now, the second Cobra starts its

run and sends four more rockets hurdling toward the ground these sounds more powerful and are as lethal as they sound. In close quarters, the have a kill range of 5 meters. Some can penetrate double and triple canopy before hitting the ground. With lethal force.

Climbing back up to 3000 feet the second cobra gets out of the way of the first and nothing, but solid rockets come flying from its wing stores. A total of 18 pairs.

Because the pilot and the gunner can see what is going on below then, they are able to access the situation and decide if additional resources are needed as well as decide if the resources should be additional AH-1G ARA Cobras or something with a bit more punch. Like an F-4 Phantom.

The cycle of diving from 3000 feet to 1500 feet continues for the next 7 minutes and then, the only thing left is the smell of exploded ordinance drifting towards your position from ground zero. Where there are now potholes where plant life and small animals called home.

After an exciting night, you get picked up and dropped off near your hooch. Thinking about eating

breakfast, you secure your TA-50 gear, lock up your camera and head to the mess hall.

Aside from what the soldiers saw that night, the ARA performs other duties such as preparing an LZ for the arrival of ground troops and protecting them while being dropped off, supporting Command and Control North activities, escorting Air Force defoliant missions and protecting VIPs such as Bob Hope and USO Shows.

Fellow soldiers you were with on guard duty appear all excited, talking faster than usual and using their hands like Cobras in the sky laying down rockets and spitting out lead through their fingers.

"Hell, of a night, buddy."

"Yeah," you say, "With that type of action going on every night, you would want to do guard duty every night."

"Heard there's a cure for that kind of thinking. Its over at corner of What Are You Insane and Psych Ward Avenue."

That put a smile on your face while pouring some coffee into the white ceramic mug.

"Listen, I've still got a couple of

shots left on the roll in the camera, why don't we take the jeep and drop by where those Cobra took off and landed. It's on our way to the PX. I can take one of you and you one of me and then I'll order two sets of prints. One for me and one for you."

"You'd do that?"

"Sure. You're the one with the jeep."

"Deal."

This type of feature is what's known as an advertorial. Its purpose intentional and clear. Show the reader the difference between the Aerial Artillery Platform verses the gunship. And then show them how it was used differently.

A regular feature of mine would start off like this:

If you are like me, chances are good you are going to be doing a lot of back packing this year.

Did you know you can lighten the weight on your back by as much as 40 percent using ultralight camping equipment?

THE FICTION ARTICLE

As mentioned previously, fiction is designed to take a character out of his normal creature-comfort zone, put him or her into a position he or she has no control over and make him work against his or her weakness.

When you first start writing fiction, because teachers seldom do discuss what I'm about to cover, the unaware of the techniques which must be used to shape a strong first paragraph and tending to focus on the main character of the story, a character sketch gets written.

The 5 o'clock alarm goes off. A hand moves through the warmth of a blanket, finds the alarm clock and turns off the alarm. Two minutes later a Preston Pierce's body comes from beneath the covers and sits in bed wearing his pajamas his mother bought him for Christmas and slips on the loafers his dad bought him that same Christmas day.

Here it comes!

After brushing his teeth, pulling out the bottle of Listerine and gargling, he stares into the mirror.

There must be a mountain the height of pulled hair equal to the height of Mount Everest.

I'm not going to save this train wreck.

The things that excite me into reading a book – a very rare occasion, I might add – is how the words shape every move with direction, description and purpose. Stopping to smell the flowers, stare into the mirror or watch the curvy creature as she wakes her nude body under the naughty blankets of your hero's sexual escapades.

WHO CARES???

"Man overboard!," "Gun!," "Fire!," "Watch out!"

These are an immature writer's way of grabbing the readers' attention.

One of the most impressive writers of my time, Irving Wallace, simply defined the main character's weakness and showed you it.

Problem is, that was the way he played his craft and the methods needed to hook the reader, no longer shine as brilliance. More like mental rape.

The meeting was unexpected. He forgot he made, he forgot he didn't cancel and he promised.

This is a typical character having a bad hair day, right?

But this character is not your typical human being, he just happens to be the new Attorney General of the United States. Not because he wanted to, but the previous owner of that title died unexpectedly.

Now, we have fiction: Through no fault of his or her own, our main character is put into a situation where he or she now must deal with being put into that situation. Unpolished, rough around the edges, the character is about to meet with someone whose about to take all of what he knows about politics and turn completely upside down.

By the way, for the record, I think 7 Minutes was Irving Wallace's best work. And I'm not going to spoil it for you.

As for me, I haven't gotten that deep into writing

one of these beasts.

But I have written 7 motorcycle related fiction articles in one day of which 5 were published. So, I think I can help in that area.

This one was called The Shovel.

With his right signal on, he powered down on his 1200 CC Harley, and shifted back to where the turn was smooth as glass. This was Youngstown, OH and a shanty looking strip bar at best. Fine red dirt kicked up behind him. Following him to where he stopped, pushed the kickstand down, turned off the lights and switched off the power.

Pulling out his cane, he began his painful walk to where it all started a year ago. The scent of stale beer, whiskey and cheap perfume replaced the smell of red dust as he went. And the sounds inside talked of drunken men and fast women.

Opening the old west style swinging doors, he saw a topless girl playing her pole and pushing her butt towards the men more than willing to shove their extra money into her G-string. A meaningless song gave her the tempo.

He studied the room and found them looking at him talking a rewind of what happened a year ago. It was the sheriff and deputy of shantytown USA. This was a red neck two with the brotherhood of 12. Some too young to know him, some too old to forget him and a few that were just too drunk to care.

This one was called ISIS.

Skunk! A little one with a broken back leg. That he saw before he lost control of his forked-out Harley, which seemed to be doing some wild horse aerial bucking of its own as his leather riding clothes absorbed much of pavement rolling he was body slamming.

He woke up to the sweetest meow he had ever heard, and the female feline was looking at him with those cute little eyes that makes you want to talk like an idiot. It rubbed his head against his arm.

He studied the cat for a moment. It did have a silver line going from the top of his head to the end of its tail. Which was why he thought it was a skunk.

Pain reminded him that his ride was pretty much trashed. He pointed to the last place he remembered his bike was doing some aerial stunts. He was glad he wasn't part of.

"You see." He started but stopped in mid-sentence. His bike was parked on the side of the road in perfect condition. Just waiting for him to get back on and ride. Thinking to himself: I have a concussion and I'm dreaming all of this up. Or I'm really seeing this and need a drink.

This one was called the Soothe Sayer. I remember this one because we were in blues and it did happen. I had to rewrite this:

"So, you're telling me not to take the job?"

"No, that's not true. I'm telling you that whether you take it or don't take it. You're a dead man. Call them, right now and tell them you don't want to steal that helicopter from Fort Polk and rob a bank with it. Tell them you are heading west on I-20."

He handed Frank a quarter, watched him dial the number and tell them exactly what his Vietnam buddy told him to say.

When he returned to the table, he picked up his keys for his motorcycle and headed out on highway I-20 west at mile marker 23, he had this sudden urge to pull over and take a leak. He was out in the open and easy picking for a fast-moving jet to run over.

Only problem is, a long-bearded man on the other side of the four lanes had a heat-seeking missile aimed at it. The bright flash and explosion caused Frank to almost guillotine his private part trying to zipper up his pants.

Frank once told this story to a bunch of Vietnam buddies he was with. They all got a good laugh from it.

"So, who was this Soothe Sayer of yours?"

"Oh, you guys remember him. Chris Carlson."

The room got deathly quiet. "You know the tall lanky one with the broken looking nose knife cut starting from just below his right eye ball. Still had that impatient finger tapping he did on the card table, too."

"Frank, Chris Carlson never came back from Nam."

"Yeah, he got sucked into one of the F-4's engines."

"Wasn't anything left of him but a puddle of blood and his ring." chimed another.

Frank pulled out the ring. "Did it look like this?"

The insignia said, "Ride with honor." The initials below, C.C.

The part I rewrote was:

"No, that's not true. I'm telling you that whether you take it or don't take it. You're a dead man. Call them, right now and tell them you don't want to steal that helicopter from Fort Polk and rob a bank with it. Tell them you are heading west on I-20."

I rewrote it to read:

"No, that's not true. I'm telling you that whether you take it or don't take it. You're a dead man. Call them, right now and tell them you don't not going to be a part of this bank heist. Tell them you are heading west on I-20."

THE SEXY SIDE OF FICTION

One of the other Writer's Groups captured my interest this morning with a sex scene that revealed age, sex, and zero experience with the opposite sex. Of course, taken out of context, it could be a memory of childhood days. One can only speculate.

What got my interest was the tempo of the movement through time and space and the choice of words which included Triumph, rack, and firm mounds which he toyed with one after the other.

Yuck!

What, was she drugged? Perhaps, she was an inflatable doll. Who knows? But one thing that was loud and clear: The author sucked at producing realism and pulled the reader away from an agreed-upon method that flows through a sex scene like a soft flowing air through the hair of female whose eyes write the stimulation a million words fail to get right.

Guys, if you're going to write a sex scene, please don't write it like you hired a hooker and you're paying for your lack of ability to understand what true romance: Not the act of two bodies engaged in the delights of each other's ability to stimulate and satisfy, but the way in which the minds of the two bodies prepare each other for the moment when the two have made themselves so stimulated by their bodies that they physically go into uncontrolled convulsions which comes with a satisfying climax.

Girls, your counter isn't a stud, while you're drunk, don't ever write a sex scene describing how you took your desire to butter him up like a butter ball turkey and put him in the oven like the witch did in Hansel and Gretel so that he turns into your own personal gingerbread man. (Even though...oh, never mind.)

Let's play the scene:

> **Peculating warmth between them was a glowing fireplace. Wine glasses half full one stained with the lips of her slightly colored lipstick.**
>
> **"I think this business proposal is firm and leaves no holes in it to be shot down by investors," she said as she pushed her hair back and way from her Norwegian face and a jaw line that suggested she was all business.**
>
> **Her dark blue eyes slightly behind those high cheekbones peering into his soul and dissecting for flaws.**
>
> **"So, we have a deal?" he asked in such a way that told her what she needed to know.**
>
> **"No." she said confidently.**
>
> **"Why not? he asked wondering what went wrong.**
>
> **"You still have your clothes on," she said in a tone that was half joking and half sincere.**

"But I'm married," he protested.

So, it begins.

How does it end?

I have no idea, I just made it up.

What I do know is I need to outline why this sexually aroused female and future business partner got into the state she was in and how the outcome will play into the reader's desire to be amused with the antics the out classed and outwitted male does caught in a woman's version of a spider's web.

Guys, resistance is futile.

Anyway, I find it to be delicious fun to see what you come – there's that word – up – there's another – with.

As for me, I must make some creamy fudge for Christmas. So, you are all on your own.

INTERVIEWING FOR PROFIT

I don't care who you are, get ready to learn from the best.

Whether it is interviewing someone for an article, a radio or TV show or just to find out what the other person on the other side of the table is thinking, it is important to remember one thing.

It isn't what you know about the person you're talking to, it's what you don't know about that person that makes the interview exciting.

Facts are facts and just hashing over them makes for some boring content and just as boring of an interview process.

TIP #1: Bring a laptop with you. Back in my day, we used notepads and 3x5 index cards we filled with questions we wanted to ask. Use the laptop to ask questions and record voice answers.

TIP #2: Start recording from the time you get out of your vehicle to the time you get back into it. The best quotes happen at the beginning and when the person being interviewed thinks the interview is over.

TIP #3: Never try to ad lib the person you interviewed or put words in his or her mouth. Not only does the dialog sound corny, you can be sued.

If you do it right, you should have all the necessary facts to build the article on before going through the interview process – the template for this is in the back of the book – and you should be able to hedge your questions based on the direction of the story.

But here's the ones I love to ask:

- Tell me more about how you went from a broke on the streets Vietnam Vet to owning this business with gross sales over 10 million.
- What was the best business decision you made – and leave the wife out of this.
- Who is your hardest customer to work with – and leave the wife out of this.
- Who is your most important customer – again, leave your wife out of this.
- How do you treat your customers differently?
- What's your proudest customer experience that you can remember?
- What was the craziest promotion you used to get customers through the door?
- What was the biggest mistake you made that you experienced and learned from? And don't use this interview as an example.
- What steps do you use to help your staff be more customer friendly?
- What techniques do you use to keep the cost of your products down?
- What's the most exciting aspect of the business for you?
- What's the most challenging?
- I see you have a lot of trophies on your wall how important is sports in your life and your children's?
- Ten years from now, when you look back. What

business strategy would you start today that would still be serving you well?

- Do you use the Internet to help you sell your products and services?
- What social medium do you find most useful? Twitter, LinkedIn, Blogs, Facebook or something else?
- What is your greatest challenge for this year? How are you addressing it?
- Where do you see yourself 7 years from now?
- Do you see your business as being the best location for your business today?
- How does the population growth in your community effect your business?
- Do you use on location radio advertising?
- What do you think advertising does for your business?
- How do you train your employees to be their best while working with your customers?
- Do you sponsor any events or activities in your community?
- What is the most important VIP that has walked through your door?
- If something would happen to you, how would this business manage?
- Do you treat your employees as family?
- What kinds of incentive programs do you have for your employees?
- Do you help them to get a higher education?
- Do you have an Employee of the Month board?
- What point of purchase strategies are you using?

- Explain why the layout of your merchandise is the way it is?
- What's the easiest part of your job?
- What is the hardest part of your job?
- How do you manage shelf life products?
- What makes your business special?
- Do you have a suggestion box?
- Do you have Android Apps that notify the customer when there is a sale on something they use?
- Do you have website how to articles that help your customers use the products and services more effectively?
- Do you ever go on vacation?
- Describe how you see yourself?
- Have you thought about bring your business to your customers?
- Do you help educate and inform the newer generation on the value and importance of your products and your services?
- What's the largest purchase ever made at your business?
- Do you have any "try me" corners?
- Do you promote art, artists and photography?
- Do you use contests to promote your business?
- Are your products seasonal? If so, how do you deal with off-season sales?
- What other businesses do you support?
- What does customer satisfaction mean to you?

I could keep on going and going. But here's the

important thing to remember, the questions you need to ask are the questions which make the story flow from one point to the next.

Two things you must remember and respect. You're taking up his or her time to talk to you. And you need to ask questions that shouldn't take 20 minutes to for him or her to answer and explain why he or she answered that way.

Here's a small example of how I work a spunky personality:

When John Gun gets up in the morning, he does what every man on this planet does. Takes a shower, gets dressed, eats breakfast with his family, kisses Martha – his wife and head off to work at his pet store. But when he's at his pet store and his customers come walking through the door, he becomes their local Buddy Hackett.

While a lady is looking at a Blue Burmese kitten, "Oh, I wouldn't buy that kitten?"

"Why not?" asks the lady.

"Look at her! She's only got one life left!" and as he walks away, "Cute little fur ball."

Reflecting on his approach, he laughs, "I've sold more kittens this way than the local SPCA. That rhymed, you know. Way, SPCA?"

My best quotes happened either while I was a bystander or right after the interviewee thought the recorder was off.

Things like:

"If there is anything I can't stand its people calling us the 3rd CAB because it sounds like CAV and CAV we are not!" said the Sergeant Major.

And:

"If you really want to know what I think about own any small business venture today, what makes the business special is what's inside the box. Inside the four walls.

"Not just the quality of the products or the services.

"You could go to Amazon and get that.

"It's the exchange between customers my sales force and met on the floor making the customer smile, treating them like human beings and making them feel special.

"And not a number on a spreadsheet."

My English teacher said I have a way with words. I also have a way with people to get those words.

Time to move on.

PHOTOJOURNALIST

What is a photojournalist? A person skilled at taking their own images and writing full length features at the same time.

Back in the latter part of the 70s and most of the 80s, if you were a photojournalist, you were a very special person. You were able to access a story and determine what would work best. This person could do the following:

- Take a picture and add to it a cut line
- Take a collection of images and write a short synopsis of what they were about
- Write a feature around some images
- Write a feature
- A cut line is a piece of paper on the back of the image that covers the date the image was taken and what is going on with the image. Suppose you took an image of a man explaining to a customer the good points of the product.
- Mark Thomas is showing a customer interested in a fish aquarium the differences between a salt-water aquarium and a fresh water aquarium at Fish Bowls Are Us, Lake Charles, LA November 1st, 2017. Picture by R. T. Edwards.
- A photo collection is basically a montage of images with cut lines and a theme. These can

be:

- A family COSPLAY wedding
- A walk around a park
- A collection of seasonal changes
- A desert collection
- A military aircraft collection
- An annual event
- A festival collection
- A travel location
- Interesting signs, lamplights or mascots collection
- An artist collection
- A photography collection
- A coin collection
- A museum collection
- A collection of model airplanes
- A visit to a zoo
- An indoor exhibition collection
- A flower collection
- A music event collection
- A group event collection
- A storefront collection
- A mime collection
- A clown collection
- A collection of elderly people
- A day in the life of collection
- A collection of civilian aircraft

The requirement here is that the collection needs a basic central theme and the images should be taken during the same time frame.

Como Park in March, Minneapolis, MN March 12th, 2017. Photos by R. T. Edwards.

The photo feature is basically a 1500 word or less feature with images that support certain highlights for the feature. The feature is themed around one of the collections above and talks more about the details of the time and place and contact information.

The full-fledged feature may have from 1 to 5 images or none and can themed around one of the many collections mentioned above along with any you can come up with on your own.

Funny thing about it is, I am 1/4th Fralinger. And if we aren't kin folk then how come so many of them are farmers in southern New Jersey and call themselves the Fralinger Brothers?

Fralinger Salt Water Taffy

Mention Salt Water Taffy and one name and place comes quickly to mind. Fralinger and The Boardwalk in Atlantic City, New Jersey.

A MAN WITH A SWEET TOOTH AND A PASSION TO BE SUCCESSFUL IS BORN

Joseph F. Fralinger (October 22, 1848 in Sweetwater – May 13, 1927 in Atlantic City, New Jersey was an American businessman and confectioner, known for being the most successful merchandiser of Salt Water Taffy. The confectionery store he founded in the late 19th century in Atlantic

City, New Jersey remains a fixture on its famous Boardwalk

HE STARTED OFF AS A GLASS BLOWER AND FISH MERCHANT

Fralinger was a glassblower and fish merchant before he opened a retail store on the Atlantic City Boardwalk to sell his taffy.

MOLASSES MADE HIM FAMOUS

Within a year, Fralinger had added a taffy concession and spent the winter perfecting the Salt Water Taffy formula, first using molasses, then chocolate and vanilla, eventually creating 25 flavors.

And of the 25 flavors, molasses is still my favorite.

The point here is threefold:

Collecting the facts about the man behind Salt Water Taffy is just as interesting as the place where the story is located.

Collecting the facts about the Boardwalk is also just as interesting as the man and the Salt Water Taffy

Collecting the facts about the history of the Salt Water Taffy is also just as interesting as the man and the boardwalk.

But there are also photo feature opportunities.

- Boardwalk sunrises
- Seashore seashells
- Romancing under the boardwalk
- Poverty behind the glamor and glitz
- Beauty of the casinos day and night

- The famous Boardwalk transportation systems.
- Cotton Candy
- Fresh Hot Pretzels
- Homemade fudge
- Birds that annoy us
- Bumper cars
- Boardwalk cops

THE PHOTO FEATURE

In the Photojournalist chapter I mentioned this kind of double-barrel approach and I mentioned this again in the Trade Publication chapter too. But mentioning it is not the same thing as showing you how to create these almost as fast as you can get home and get 1500 words to sail across the pages.

The first thing you must do is have an organized plan of attack.

This is a story about a (fictitious) bicycle shop with the content targeted for a trade publication that uses business store profiles.

> The first thing to hit your senses is the energy the puppets have greeting you at the door. Wait, did I just say puppets?
>
> "It's funny how much those puppets really make this bicycle shop come alive," Robert Redford, owner of Cyclic Styles reflected. "How many stores have Mickey Mouse or Donald Duck meeting you at the door while riding a bicycle, saying hello and welcome to Cyclic Styles and when you leave, hands you a packet of discounts, quality information about bicycling, and maps on bicycling routes with Daffy Duck saying, something corny?"
>
> Robert Redford, age 32, has always been interested in cartoon characters and

has always had a passion for bicycling. So, it only makes sense for the two interests to blend into ... well, Cyclic Styles.

Compared to most bicycle shops, this one is larger and more defined.

There is a place where his customers can drink some Starbucks coffee, check their e-mail and go through the hundreds of articles on a variety of subjects and categories covering the bicycle lifestyle while waiting for their chance to talk with a floor sales representative. On the other side of the shop is a similar area where new bicycles are built, and ones that needed repair are picked up.

Redford pointed out, "Our customer experience is crucial to the success of the business. We can't keep customers if you don't offer bicycle and bicycle related products and services with an experience level above and beyond what our customers would get elsewhere.

"We are the bar by which other shops must compete against and we constantly raise it."

But there is something else going on behind the scenes that also adds to this bar raising. Something that few other competitors would dare to do. For every event they come to, he credits his customers $12.50 of the $25 for each event they attend to go back towards a new bicycle.

"The idea here is they are seeing funds they can use on a retail. That is always higher than what I pay, so, it is good for everyone involved," reflected Redford. "I have 52 events each year. Street tours and off-road experiences. If they join the club for $100, they get awards for the number of miles they ride every quarter and year.

"We have leader boards and a website with the same information on them."

But Redford doesn't hold a line in the sand with respect to walking enthusiasts as well as kayakers.

"We have areas on the second floor for these interests, too. And we've included outdoor camping equipment, which may not have the same profit levels as the bicycle shop business but does enable our customers to see, understand, and appreciate the entire spectrum of the bicycling lifestyle.

"The beauty of nature is to be out in nature and feel comfortable and secure in the process. Providing them with incentives such as reward programs and up close and personal customer support is my best way of showing them how the complete lifestyle will enrich their family's experiences together is a really big win for me."

Also, up on the second floor is an area where the children learn safety through puppets and a member of the local police force.

"The kids really get a big laugh out of Sylvester getting a ticket for not wearing his helmet and then gets thrown into Tweety Bird's bird cage. And then Tweety Bird scolds him for being a wreely baad putty cat.

"It's laughter with some serious safety information, too. Safety, after all is my highest Priority."

There are some stationary bikes near the build and repair area too, but they aren't there to be on display to sell them.

Instead, they are there to showcase the various products and services Redford's employees or local programmers have created that are designed to "keep the bottom in the seat."

"Do you know how many calories are in a pound of fat? 3,500. At the rate of burning 300 per hour, you would have to work the pedals of some stationary bicycles for close to 12 hours a day.

"The fact is, roughly a pound and a half a week is doable. But it needs to be made interesting and fun. So, the first thing we looked at was the issue with the east on these machines. So, I contacted a local seamstress and suggested that if she could come up with some cool and comfortable seat cushions for them, I would put them on the stationary bikes and on my website and, well, the rest is history.

"I did the same for a couple of programmers who have been able to combine a reasonable weight loss program with the stationary bike routines and a program that would take this information and place it on a leader board.

"Our top weeklies get a Starbucks card and monthlies get free movie passes. Quarterlies get to raffle for a new bicycle and our yearlies get a free trip to Europe.

"The programmers get paid $35 of the $50 annual sales and we use the rest to cover the incentives. So, it is a win, win, win for everyone"

All well and good, but three things which appear to be left unanswered is how does he find the time to do all of this, what happens during seasonal conditions and what types of advertising does he do?

"The reason why all of this works isn't because me. I simply come up with solutions that resolve problems for my customers. The rest is done by my staff. The way I see it, if I died tomorrow, it would take this business 7 years before one of my managers would have to take the bull by the horns and make the decisions I'm making today.

"The point I'm trying to make here is that good management is when the main manager can walk out the door and the business will keep running without an issue because the assistant managers work together as a team.

"We're not perfect and we know it and I leave it to my senior staff members to manage their departments. When they find an area that needs to be discussed and worked on, they do it.

"Unless they're talking about making major changes to the shop, I don't get involved.

"As for taking a vacation, I take that with my customers who win the trip overseas. I show them a good time over there, let them enjoy the experience and we take a bicycle ride together and that gets filmed. Everyone has a good time. I call it funtising.

"We haven't talked about advertising for a good reason. Advertising costs money and that money could be spent on other things that makes the shop fun and exciting to make purchases through. You can't make a profit from selling bicycles at retail if the profit margin is eaten up by the overhead of advertising.

"A lot of my time is spent on taking my business to potential customers. I'd rather do that than having to spend the same money on advertising. I think the effect is more personal and upbeat.

"There are 20,000 people in this town, a $2,000 dollar per month advertisement is

$1.20 per citizen.

"Three-fourths of that are children, retirees and people who just don't like bicycles and a bicycling lifestyle.

"Now, you're now down to 7,500. The actual number of people who walk through the door who are not added when they are repeat annual sales is 300 per month. That's now $6.67 per person. That's a lazy man's way of getting 300 people through the door.

"So, I go to the schools. I do talks about bicycle safety. I go to the local newspaper and provide them with interesting stories about the people who work for me. I take out ads in them when I have something on sale that attracts a crowd. I work with the bicycle manufacturers and allow them to showcase their newest products. I go to the mayor's office and the town meetings to get approval for designated bicycle routes.

"But what really works for me is word-of-mouth advertising."

"That comes as no surprise considering the massive amount of effort put into impressing the minute he or she comes walking through the door and the moment they leave with a smile on their face."

But what made front-page news from this writer's perspective was the honesty and the integrity of the staff that works there. If there is a weak link in this shop's

> chain of strengths, it certainly isn't obvious.
>
> Even the area where the new bicycles are built and repaired. With 6 open bays where the customers can view the progress through plexiglass windows speaks in volume about the professional work being accomplished by staff members whom themselves are bicyclists.
>
> Without a doubt, Cyclic Styles is a bicycle shop that lives up to its name and reputation.

Normally, I wouldn't spend this much time writing a totally bogus feature like this, but I wanted to show you how a story like this one – even though it is totally fictitious – can be put together based on very specific highlights.

There are:

- Puppets
- Layout
- Second floor
- Promotions
- Advertisements
- Bicycle building and repair
- Reputation

Now, think about this for a minute. Seven points at 200 words = 1400 words. Transitions between the various images that need to be taken to make this story real take up an additional 100 words.

Promotions and advertisements are images, too. It's the signs in the buildings, the information stations and the visuals that depict the personality of the business.

Here's the same story for a business opportunity publication:

> Robert Redford, age 32, doesn't just tell you his bicycle shop, cyclic styles, he shows you from the time you open the door to the time you leave. The first thing to hit your senses is the energy the puppets have greeting you at the door. Wait, did I just say puppets?
>
> "It's funny how much those puppets really make this bicycle shop come alive," Robert Redford, owner of cyclic styles reflected. "How many stores have Mikey Mouse or Donald Duck meeting you at the door while riding a bicycle, saying hello and welcome to Cyclic Styles and when you leave, hands you a packet of discounts, quality information about bicycling and maps on bicycling routes with Daffy Duck saying, something corny?"
>
> Robert Redford, age 32, has always been interested in cartoon characters and has always had a passion for bicycling. So, it only makes sense for the two interests to blend into...well, cyclic styles.
>
> Compared to most bicycle shops, this one is larger and more defined.
>
> There is a place where his customers can drink some Starbucks coffee, check their e-mail and go through the hundreds of

articles on a variety of subjects and categories covering the bicycle lifestyle while waiting for their chance to talk with a floor sales representative. On the other side of the shop is a similar area where new bicycles are built, and ones needed repair are picked up.

Redford, pointed out, "Our customer experience is crucial to the success of the business. We can't keep customers if you don't offer bicycle and bicycle related products and services with an experience level above and beyond what our customers would get elsewhere.

"We are the bar by which other shops must compete against and we constantly raise it."

But there is something else going on behind the scenes that also adds to this bar raising. Something that few other competitors would dare to do. For every event they come to, he credits his customers $12.50 of the $25 for each event they come to back towards a new bicycle.

"The idea here is they are seeing funds they can use on a retail. That is always higher than what I pay, so, it is good for everyone involved," reflected Redford. "I have 52 events each year. Street tours, and off-road experiences. If they join the club for $100, they get awards for the number of miles they ride every quarter and year.

"We have leader boards and a website with the same information on them."

But Redford doesn't hold a line in the sand with respect to walking enthusiasts as well as kayakers.

"We have areas on the second floor for these interests, too. And we've included outdoor camping equipment which may not have the same profit levels with the bicycle shop business but does enable our customers to see, understand and appreciate the entire spectrum of the bicycle lifestyle.

The beauty of nature is to be out in nature and feel comfortable and secure in the process. Providing them with incentives such as reward programs and up close and personal customer support is my best way of showing them how the complete lifestyle will enrich their family's experiences together is a really big win for me."

Also, up on the second floor is an area where the children learn safety through puppets and one of the local police force.

"The kids really get a big laugh out of Sylvester getting a ticket for not wearing his helmet and then gets thrown into Tweety Bird 's bird cage. And then Tweety Bird scolds him for being a wreely baad putty cat.

"It's laughter with some serious safety information, too. Safety, after all is my highest Priority."

There are some stationary bikes near the build and repair area too, but they aren't there to be on display to sell them.

Instead, they are there to showcase the various products and services Redford's employees or local programmers have created that are designed to "keep the bottom in the seat."

"Do you know how many calories are in a pound of fat? 3,500. At the rate of burning 300 per hour, you would have to work the pedals of some stationary bicycles for close to 12 hours a day.

"The fact is, roughly a pound and a half a week is doable. But it needs to be made interesting and fun. So, the first thing we looked at was the issue with the east on these machines. So, I contacted a local seamstress and suggested to her that if she could come up with some cool and comfortable seat cushions for them, I would put them on the stationary bikes and on my website and, well, the rest is history.

"I did the same for a couple of programmers who have been able to combine a reasonable weight loss program, combined it with the stationary bike routines and a program that would take this information and place it on a leader board.

Our top weeklies get a Starbucks card and monthlies get free movie passes. Quarterlies get to raffle for a new bicycle and our year lies get a free trip to Europe.

"The programmers get paid $35 of the $50 annual sales and we use the rest to cover the incentives. So, it is a win, win, win for everyone"

All well and good, but three things which appear to be left unanswered is how does he find the time to do all of this, what happens during seasonal conditions and what types of advertising does he do?

"The reason why all of this works isn't because me. I simply come up with solutions that resolve problems for my customers. The rest is done by my staff. The way I see it, if I died tomorrow, it would take this business 7 years before one of my managers would have to take the bull by the horns and make the decisions I'm making today.

"The point I'm trying to make here is that good management is when the main manager can walk out the door and the business will keep running with an issue because the assistant managers work together as a team.

"We're not perfect and we know it and I leave it to my senior staff members to manage their departments. When they find an area that needs to be discussed and worked on, they do it.

"Unless they're talking about making major changes to the shop, I don't get involved.

"As for taking a vacation, I take that with my customers who win the trip overseas. I show them a good time over there, let them enjoy the experience and we take a bicycle ride together and that gets filmed. Everyone has a good time. I call it funtising.

"We haven't talked about advertising for a good reason. Advertising costs money and that money could be spent on other things that makes the shop fun and exciting to make purchases through. You can't make a profit from selling bicycles at retail if the profit margin is eaten up by the overhead of advertising.

"A lot of my time is spent on taking my business to potential customers. I'd rather do that than having to spend the same money on advertising. I think the effect is more personal and upbeat.

"There are 20,000 people in this town, a $2,000 dollar per month advertisement is $1.20 per citizen.

"Three-fourths of that are children, retirees and people who just don't like bicycles and a bicycling lifestyle.

"Now, you're now down to 7,500. The actual number of people who walk through the door who are not added when they are repeat annual sales is 300 per month. That's now $6.67 per person. That's a lazy man's way of getting 300 people through the door.

"So, I go to the schools. I do talks about bicycle safety. I go to the local newspaper and provide them with interesting stories about the people who work for me. I take out ads in them when I have something on sale that attracts a crowd. I work with the bicycle manufacturers and allow them to showcase their newest products. I go to the mayor's office and the town meetings to get approval for designated bicycle routes.

"But what really works for me is by word of mouth advertising."

That comes as no surprise considering the massive amount of effort put into impressing the minute he or she comes walking through the door and the moment they leave with a smile on their face.

But what made front-page news from this writer's perspective was the honesty and the integrity of the staff that works there. If there is a weak link in this shops chain of strengths, it certainly isn't obvious.

Even the area where the new bicycles are built and repaired. With 6 open bays where the customers can view the progress through plexiglass windows speaks in volume about the professional work being accomplished by staff members whom themselves are bicyclists.

And here's one for a local newspaper:

Robert Redford, age 32, doesn't just tell you his bicycle shop, cyclic styles, he shows you from the time you open the door to the time you leave. The first thing to hit your senses is the energy the puppets have greeting you at the door. Wait, did I just say puppets?

"It's funny how much those puppets really make this bicycle shop come alive," Robert Redford, owner of cyclic styles reflected. "How many stores have Mikey Mouse or Donald Duck meeting you at the door while riding a bicycle, saying hello and welcome to Cyclic Styles and when you leave, hands you a packet of discounts, quality information about bicycling and maps on bicycling routes with Daffy Duck saying, something corny?"

Robert Redford, age 32, has always been interested in cartoon characters and has always had a passion for bicycling. So, it only makes sense for the two interests to blend into...well, cyclic styles.

Compared to most bicycle shops, this one is larger and more defined.

There is a place where his customers can drink some Starbucks coffee, check their e-mail and go through the hundreds of articles on a variety of subjects and categories covering the bicycle lifestyle while waiting for their chance to talk with a floor sales representative. On the other side of the shop is a similar area where new bicycles are built, and ones needed repair are picked up.

Redford, pointed out, "Our customer experience is crucial to the success of the business. We can't keep customers if you don't offer bicycle and bicycle related products and services with an experience level above and beyond what our customers would get elsewhere.

"We are the bar by which other shops must compete against and we constantly raise it."

But there is something else going on behind the scenes that also adds to this bar raising. Something that few other competitors would dare to do. For every event they come to, he credits his customers $12.50 of the $25 for each event they come to back towards a new bicycle.

"The idea here is they are seeing funds they can use on a retail. That is always higher than what I pay, so, it is good for everyone involved," reflected Redford. "I have 52 events each year. Street tours, and off-road experiences. If they join the club for $100, they get awards for the number of miles they ride every quarter and year.

"We have leader boards and a website with the same information on them."

But Redford doesn't hold a line in the sand with respect to walking enthusiasts as well as kayakers.

"We have areas on the second floor for these interests, too. And we've included outdoor camping equipment, which may not have the same profit levels with the bicycle shop business but does enable our customers to see, understand and appreciate the entire spectrum of the bicycle lifestyle.

The beauty of nature is to be out in nature and feel comfortable and secure in the process. Providing them with incentives such as reward programs and up close and personal customer support is my best way of showing them how the complete lifestyle will enrich their family's experiences together is a really big win for me."

Also, up on the second floor is an area where the children learn safety through puppets and one of the local police force.

"The kids really get a big laugh out of Sylvester getting a ticket for not wearing his helmet and then gets thrown into Tweety Bird 's bird cage. And then Tweety Bird scolds him for being a wreely baad putty cat.

"It's laughter with some serious safety information, too. Safety, after all is my highest Priority."

There are some stationary bikes near the build and repair area too, but they aren't there to be on display to sell them.

Instead, they are there to showcase the various products and services Redford's employees or local programmers have created that are designed to "keep the bottom in the seat."

"Do you know how many calories are in a pound of fat? 3,500. At the rate of burning 300 per hour, you would have to work the pedals of some stationary bicycles for close to 12 hours a day.

"The fact is, roughly a pound and a half a week is doable. But it needs to be made interesting and fun. So, the first thing we looked at was the issue with the east on these machines. So, I contacted a local seamstress and suggested to her that if she could come up with some cool and comfortable seat cushions for them, I would put them on the stationary bikes and on my website and, well, the rest is history.

"I did the same for a couple of programmers who have been able to combine a reasonable weight loss program, combined it with the stationary bike routines and a program that would take this information and place it on a leader board.

Our top weeklies get a Starbucks card and monthlies get free movie passes. Quarterlies get to raffle for a new bicycle and our year lies get a free trip to Europe.

"The programmers get paid $35 of the

$50 annual sales and we use the rest to cover the incentives. So, it is a win, win, win for everyone"

All well and good, but three things which appear to be left unanswered is how does he find the time to do all of this, what happens during seasonal conditions and what types of advertising does he do?

"The reason why all of this works isn't because me. I simply come up with solutions that resolve problems for my customers. The rest is done by my staff. The way I see it, if I died tomorrow, it would take this business 7 years before one of my managers would have to take the bull by the horns and make the decisions I'm making today.

"The point I'm trying to make here is that good management is when the main manager can walk out the door and the business will keep running with an issue because the assistant managers work together as a team.

"We're not perfect and we know it and I leave it to my senior staff members to manage their departments. When they find an area that needs to be discussed and worked on, they do it.

"Unless they're talking about making major changes to the shop, I don't get involved.

"As for taking a vacation, I take that

with my customers who win the trip overseas. I show them a good time over there, let them enjoy the experience and we take a bicycle ride together and that gets filmed. Everyone has a good time. I call it funtising. Speaking of advertising, when Robert was asked what kinds of advertising he uses, he said, "The only form of advertising is by word of mouth.

"Look around you, do I really need more?"

If you are not like me, chances are good you are not mechanically inclined. So, when it comes down to purchasing a bicycle that needs to be built, who you going to call?

Cyclic Styles, that's who.

His shop builds many of all bicycles parent purchase throughout the city for free. Yes, that's right, for free.

"While we do ask for donations that goes to the local men's shelter, anyone can bring in a bicycle that needs to be built and we'll build it."

But there is another reason why the Robert wants people to come to Cyclic Styles to get their bicycles built and that's bad publicity.

"Ride safe, ride with integrity," remarked Robert. "That's not just a motto, that is our reputation. One child that gets hurt riding a bicycle, the public automatically wants to blame the parents and then the bicycle shop.

"And that's something we can't have over our heads. Besides, when they have a chance to see their bicycle get built in front of their eyes, they know the work exceeds their expectations. We pride ourselves on building the bicycles to specs.

"We'll even tell the customer to return the bicycle if its poorly built and its life expectancy is about a day after it goes out the door."

The area where the new bicycles are built and repaired has 6 open bays. Customers can view the progress through plexiglass windows. And that speaks in volumes about the professional work being accomplished by staff members. All of whom are avid bicyclists.

WRITING FOR TRADES

Why write for trades? After all, what do you know about Army/Navy Surplus, Pet Shops, Massage businesses, Chiropractic business or for the matter, Basket Weaving?

Well, that's exactly the reasons why you should. Because you have more of a chance to get published here than other publications and the average check from these is around 10 cents per word than 5 cents per word.

Convinced?

Got to be a catch?

Nope.

While the book is 20 years old, Stephen Wagner put together a book from many writers who wrote for him including myself. It is called *Mind Your Own Business*. It is full of great articles and work that could sell today with a modern and up to date slant.

Okay, so what can you write for trades that you can feel comfortable doing?

Well, for one thing you can go to various stores throughout your area and find ones that are doing well and then ask them for a copy of the publications they read, leave a business card and then see what kinds of articles they use.

Many like doing profiles of businesses throughout the world that are inspirational and have equally interesting business owners.

You may also find tones of ideas from articles that way.

In the previous chapter, we talked about the art of interview. The processes and steps in that section making it easier to create copy that will help you sell your work. I have been, and I always will be one of the best interviewers that was ever put on this planet.

Beyond the human interest stories or day in the life of stories, hard hitting, short and sweet and to the point – what I call "wake up call" features – drive home a particular fact about business essentials – such as communications, point of sales, marketing techniques and advertising campaigns and promotional strategies that are timeless and effective reminders for business owners and managers to consider.

So, what can you write for trade publications?

- Just how effective is your business card?
- Selling from The Heart.
- When no is yes with a question unanswered.
- Objections are proof you sales pitch didn't work.
- When a pushy sales force kills your profit line.
- Where is your sweet spot?
- Why "I doubt it" is such a hard customer response.
- Have you tried on location radio advertising?
- Why advertising doesn't always have to draw in customers.
- How to take advantage of seasonal trends.
- 5 incentive programs that boots sales
- Your weakest link is what you should work on
- How news releases can promote the business

- Why visual effects can sell more products and services
- Piped in music can make or break your business
- There's no business-like show business
- How one popular item on the shelf can sell others with higher profit margins
- When promoting your employees works in your favor.
- The art of a cold sell.
- Just how computer techie is you?
- Communications is a two-way street.
- Supporting local talent adds to business visibility.
- Do you have a local community booster club?
- Have a garage sale!
- Walls empty? Showcase local artist's talent.
- Hire a national celebrity to promote your business.
- Sponsor a battle of the bands.
- Sell your business to high school and college graduates.
- Take your business on the road.
- Its gadget month, have you a gadget no one else does that everyone wants?
- Turn profit on selling used games.
- Sponsor child bicycle safety awareness.
- Save the kittens! Work with local vets.
- Volunteering at homeless kitchens can be a very interesting and newsworthy experience.
- Get to know your customers better.

- Sponsor a Vietnam Vet.
- Up for a photo contest?
- How turns work.
- Have National Guard or Reservists working for you? Show them you care.
- It's a Starbucks invasion!
- Promote recycling.
- It's Marvel Mania Day!
- Sponsor and support a local theater show no matter how bad the cast is!
- Improve your Marketing skills using these 3 easy steps.
- Sharpen your Advertising skills.
- When liars knock on your door.
- When a sales pitch sounds solid and true.
- What's an advertorial?
- How to sell Eskimos ice cubes.
- Free $15 box of chocolates for every 15 customers who purchase a product on Valentine's Day.
- Sponsor a free walking event.

When Chris Powel is not enough, the book, *Mind Your Own Business* will help you write the articles.

THE ART OF WRITING SHORT SCIENCE FICTION STORIES

Is it possible to write short story Science Fiction without sounding like a Science teacher or someone with a degree in political science?

The answer is yes. But let's first define what Science Fiction is verses Fantasy Fiction.

Science Fiction is the art of weaving a plot into a marvelous different world then the world we live in whereas Fantasy Fiction is the art of weaving a plot into a past, present or future world based on some sort of calamity that happened on this world in the past, present or future.

Star Wars, Star Trek, Enemy Mine are Science Fiction. *Lord of The Rings, Harry Potter, Merlin* are Fantasy.

But both share the similar plotting strategies good must overcome evil. Both genres offer post twists.

For example, *Enemy Mine* puts two fighter pilots who are from opposing worlds onto a world where the two must depend on each other, so they can survive on a hostile planet.

Then there's the religious based three characters – the two opposites always personifying the weaknesses or strengths of the main character whose god like intuition somehow manages to survive with the two with or without his ship or all members of his crew intact.

Harry Potter is also based on three main characters and both systems of characters are designed for more than one book or show.

The idea behind formula writing is the writer hopes to lure you in with emotional stimulus that brands the work. After all, it is your investment of money and time you are investing to be swept away into the characters' world on a planet far, far away.

It is through high-octane characters and their personal relationships with each other that you relate to and be whisked away from reality. This coupled with a satisfying ending hints you are wanting more.

This is what novels are all about. But short stories regardless of genre haven't the luxury of romancing you into believable characters. In fact, these rely on the fight is on between good and evil the instant the story starts to unfold.

Then there's the notion of literally Science Fiction and Fantasy writing. And I am the first to admit that I wasn't ready to deal with it at that level. I am now.

Here's an example of with is meant, I just told a certain writer's flock to basically leave him alone. At the literary level, it would look like this:

Whisper quietly oh gentle fold of o be ones. Whilst his gray matter of highly organized thoughts flow like a spring against the dark side of drought and doubt, we must silence our ourselves until the work is mastered and we wonder in amazement how the blood of living breathing tissue set us upon a path of ink laced chosen words in spell binding order. Quenching our desire to be amazed.

As for the question posed at the very beginning: Is it possible to write short story Science Fiction without sounding like a science teacher or someone with a degree in political science?

The answer is yes and the films and stories I've selected prove it.

SOMETHING WICKED THIS WAY COMES

Think about this line:

> *The mystery of the object hanging motionlessly in the silence of the air shrouded in the mist. Humans asking questions: why here, why now.*

Obviously, this intro involves an alien craft and could be one of many movies about aliens entering our world as far back as I can remember. But this line is normally not the first line you expect to be used in an intro.

But alright, I'm using it as an example as why this line needs to be polished up. First off, I have a bunch of prepositional phrases:

of the object
in the silence
of the air
in the mist
asking questions

Let's try fixing it:

> *Hanging in silence just above the ground. It was dull and lacked detail. In short, the skin of the craft provided none of the human senses with any stimuli that evoked danger or salvation.*

> *Lacking the human stimulation for fight or flight, the void silence invoked the questions of why here, why now.*
>
> *"If it isn't from the earth we can only assume to things. This is going to be a really exciting time for humans on this planet or we can kiss our asses goodbye."*

I just had to add that last line. Okay, by now, you've already figured out the specific movie I'm dancing around the fire with that is Arrival.

Let's summarize. A woman who's very good with languages is about to have her brain rewired by telepathic time travelers who must steer humans' violent and aggressive nature and channel that into a higher level of thought. When they return 3000 years in the future, their language, the math and the technology advancements created – including telepathic development – will be understood and they will be able to live in harmony with humans.

There are a lot of audience cues that talk of the theory that language shapes the way we think.

I for one know that this is true. I've experienced that myself after having to learn German and communicate in German while stationed in Germany. My writing skills improved tenfold.

But do you see the problem here?

First, the movie tries to show us a past that hasn't yet happened and a present that says it has. Then we get to the end of the movie where she must use her telepathic powers to convince a Chinese military leader that she knows what his wife said on her deathbed and adverts a confrontation between the aliens and the Chinese.

While this movie did well, I believe it did so because it carries with it a significant and at the same time troubling association with the Catholic religion. 12 ships, 12 apostles. Each carrying a different message. And only she can unravel the mystery.

Religion has this thing about telepathic women. They are generally burned at the stake. I'm pretty sure her husband would be the first in line to light the wood under her feet.

Not because she told him the truth but because humans live on the earth and not in the air. At least, not yet. And in all honesty, where this movie left off is where this movie should have started.

Visual Themes:

- Twelve Ships
- Alpha\Omega
- Human Evolution
- Trinity
- Blind Acceptance
- Virgin Mary Syndrome
- Blind Acceptance
- Kill the Aliens
- One word wrongly interrupted
- Greed
- Jesus will return
- Has the government ever told the truth?

You can't get much more religious than that. Made 230 million worldwide. The new SOLO is going to make that much in 1 week. The powers to be proclaimed it to be one of the top 25 Alien Invasions Movies. In my life, there have only been 3 involving space ships.

War of The Worlds
Independence Day
Arrival

The rest either didn't come here in a space ships or were B Movie spinoffs.

Last thoughts:

If there is a higher intelligence outside beyond of feeble intelligence of greed and hatred towards each other has overcome, they would describe humans as a global killer. As a species unable to tolerate its own minorities and define them as organisms that destroyed its own existence for the sake of greed, power and senseless wars. And it would be summed up as "over breeding planet killers."

But there is light at the end of the tunnel. A new generation of generations to come has arrived. Not by alien spaceships but by cross breeding the high-energy genetic pool from India with extremely smart American women. The outcome will cross the 3000 AD timeline with an explosion of changes exceeding anything seen on this planet.

Done.

The reason why I even brought this piece of trash up in the first place was to prove a couple of very important points. Anyone with an active imagination can create event driven circumstances that can put any person into a state of peril that he or she has no control over.

- You wake up and the entire world has been turned upside down.
- You wake up and you realize your day has come where eternity is forever.
- You wake up and you realize you are the opposite sex.
- You wake up and you're back in time when you're Merlin.
- You wake up and you're back in time when you're dealing with a dragon.
- You wake up and you're back in time when you're up to your neck in mud and sinking fast.
- You wake up and your back in time when you're up to your neck in tar and people are still placing bets.
- You wake up and you're back in time when you're up to a noose around your neck.
- You wake up and your back in time when you're a black slave being whipped.
- You wake up and you're back in time when you're James Bond in Gold finger.
- You wake up and you're back in time when you're Hans Christen Anderson.
- You wake up and you're back in time when you're Shakespeare.
- You wake up and you're back in time when you're a droid.
- You wake up and you're back in time when you're a gladiator.
- You wake up and you're back in time when you're a Pirate.

- You wake up and you're back in time when you're a black leopard.
- You wake up and you're back in time when you're a gladiator.
- You wake up and your back in time when you're a knight in shining armor.
- You wake up and you're in current time and you are Merlin.
- You wake up and you're in current time and you are dealing with a dragon.
- You wake up and you're in current time and you are up to your neck in mud and sinking fast.
- You wake up and you're in current time and you are up to your neck in tar and people are still placing bets.
- You wake up and you're in current time and you are up to a noose around your neck.
- You wake up and you're in current time and you are a black slave being whipped.
- You wake up and you're in current time and you are a girl painting James Bond gold.
- You wake up and you're in current time and you are Hans Christen Anderson.
- You wake up and you're in current time and you are Shakespeare.
- You wake up and you're in current time and you are a droid.
- You wake up and you're in current time and you are a gladiator.
- You wake up and you're in current time and you are a Pirate.

- You wake up and you're in current time and you are a black leopard.
- You wake up and you're in current time and you are a gladiator.
- You wake up and you're in current time and you are a knight in shining armor.
- You wake up and the world is 2000 years older.
- You wake up and your future time and you are Merlin.
- You wake up and your future time and you are dealing with a dragon.
- You wake up and your future time and you are up to your neck in mud and sinking fast.
- You wake up and your future time and you are up to your neck in tar and people are still placing bets.
- You wake up and your future time and you are up to a noose around your neck.
- You wake up and your future time and you are a black slave being whipped.
- You wake up and your future time and you are painted gold.
- You wake up and your future time and you are Hans Christen Anderson.
- You wake up and your future time and you are Shakespeare.
- You wake up and your future time and you are a droid.
- You wake up and your future time and you are a gladiator.
- You wake up and your future time and you are a

Pirate.

- You wake up and your future time and you are a black leopard.
- You wake up and your future time and you are a gladiator.
- You wake up and your future time and you are a knight in shining armor.
- You wake up, go down to the local ATM machine and it says f**k you.
- You get into your car and go to your local convenience store and the mist rolls in.
- You get into your car and you fall asleep at the wheel.
- You get into your car and it turns into a giant robot.
- You get into your car and it turns into a time machine.
- You get into your car and it blows up in your face.
- You get into your car and a guy with a gun tells you to drive.
- You get into your car and a girl with a can of mace tells you to drive.
- You get into your car and a dog starts talking to you.
- You get into your car and a cat starts talking to you.
- You get into your car and you hit another car at 75 miles per hour.
- You get into your car and everything around you begins to shake violently.
- You get into your car and you're in the front seat

of a flying machine.

- You get into your car and it sends you to jail.
- You get into your car and you get buried alive in a sinkhole.
- You get into your car and you hit another car at 75 miles per hour.
- You're in an airplane, it flies onto a cloud and the next thing you know, you're on a different planet
- You're in an airplane, and it crashes back in time.
- You're in an airplane, and it never lands
- You marry a witch
- You marry a spy
- You marry a hooker
- You marry superman
- You marry superwoman
- You marry a soldier with a dark and forbidden past
- You marry mister stupid
- You marry a genius with no common sense
- You marry a stalker
- You marry a cereal box hero
- You marry a newspaper ad
- You marry mister wrong for all the right reasons
- You meet an alien
- You are an alien
- You are a witch
- You are a spy
- You are a hooker
- You are superman
- You are superwoman

- You are a soldier with a dark and forbidden past
- You are mister stupid
- You are a genius with no common sense
- You are a stalker
- You are a cereal box hero
- You are the average man or woman who's gifted with special powers
- You are the gift humanity needs to use to survive.
- You go to work at a library where the books come a live at night
- You go to work at a museum where the artifacts take you back in time to solve a mystery or save the day
- You go to work where the museum comes alive at night
- You go to work as a janitor at a school where the school heroes walk the halls at night
- You know something is going to happen before it happens, and you don't know why.
- When taking a chance goes right for all the wrong reasons.

Do these things sound familiar? Some ought to because some have been turned into movies. TV shows and millions of books. They are timeless, too. I could take anyone of these and spin a short story out of each one of them.

FACTION

It's also something I'm really, good at.

Fiction is designed to take a character out of his normal creature comfort zone, put him or her into a position he or she has no control over and make him work against his or her weakness.

Pretty simple, right? Throw someone in the deep end of a pool and tell him or her to sink or swim.

Well, it is a bit more complex than that for the following reasons:

You know the person will be saved otherwise you could go to jail for attempted murder

You know the outcome will be the person learns how to swim or the person gets saved

Unless it is a person you care about or is someone you don't know but respect his or her status, the story becomes boring and trite.

The third one explains why the guy or girl next door isn't the main character. Unless the main character in the story is played by a movie icon such as Bruce Willis and you know that movie star doesn't play second string. Plus, the name of the movie is RED.

Literary fiction – especially the shorts – deals with the following:

- Morality verses Immorality
- Socialization verses anti-socialization
- Sane verses insane
- Discipline verses Psychotic behavior

- Normal verses abnormal
- Religion verses ant-religion

But in faction, the fiction tools of drama are used to pull the reader into the story. It must perform the following:

- Cause the drama
- Set the stage of chance into motion
- Provide the reader with a sense of struggle that may or may not be resolved
- Lock the reader's attention within 8 seconds.
- Use a quote to summarize the frustration
- Offer a sense that things might be changing.

My first article I wrote for *EurArmy Magazine* went like this:

> The fog was so thick you could cut it with a knife. A whiff of warmth touched the soldiers as the door opened and a pair of hands extends some steamy black *esprit de corps* to the guards. "Today is the day were going to go hot, I can feel it in my bones."
>
> The sheet of dense fog had the 3rd Combat Aviation Battalion, 3rd Infantry Division weathered in.
>
> The battalion was on a training exercise at Hohenfels, Germany and this was day 3 of a 5-day time slot. And they were just hankering for a chance to fire off some Tube Launched, Optically Tracked, Wire Guided TOW missiles at some armor targets.

This wasn't as cool as the original because I don't have the original and I have also learned not to make the work sound so corny, more dramatic and the fiction flowing at a much faster pace.

But more importantly focused on a target audience, quenching their thirst for speed and performance.

"Say your prayers," said the front seat pilot trained to mark and follow the target to this exact moment when three 6-foot-long titanium rods dove themselves through the side of the tank instantly heating the insides including the ammo and occupants to 3000 degrees Fahrenheit. "Karma is a bitch."

I want to do a few more for recreational publications.

It was big, it was hairy, and it was uninvited. Two city slickers were about to get a wakeup call they would learn a valuable lesson from. Spectators rallied around the early morning campfire sipping coffee. Placing bets on what was about to happen next.

If you had the desire to want to read more, so did I. Wasn't that the point?

10 a.m., May 25th, 2016. A man from Louisiana and a friend head up a poorly maintained trail. About halfway up, a swarm of Africanized Killer Bees from out of nowhere decides this was the day this 270-pound man

would die from 1,000 bee stings.

On the night of May 24th, 2016, I was walking on the Merkle Trail that is divided by the Vista Trail five times to get my five miles in as part of my physical exercise program.

If that doesn't get you interested, you're dead. Okay, last one.

> "Did you hear that," asked my wife.
>
> "Hear what."
>
> "Shush." she commanded.
>
> "The sound was distant but clear who owned it. I pulled out my binoculars. Coiled up 30 feet on the trail was a good-sized rattlesnake out in the open. The scream of an Eagle sailing high above us had me pulling out my camera and tripod and focusing on the snake."
>
> "What, exactly are you doing?" she asked like our lives were at stake here and you're taking pictures!
>
> "I called the animal control psychic hot line and they told me that in less than 10 minutes the trail would be clear. Told me to take pictures of the event because they might just be the COVER for *National Geographic*."
>
> "Dreamer!"
>
> "Yeah, I hear I married one, too."

While not so dramatic, the images would have taken up the slack.

BUSINESS PROFILES

Past or present, business profiles. I did this one on an old theater in Moorestown, NJ:

> Almost everyone these days goes to very clean, modern, and acoustically finetuned movie theaters that seem to spend 15 minutes forcing you to watch trailers or video advertisements or both before getting to the reason why you came to the theater in the first place: "the main attraction."
>
> It wasn't always this way. In fact, back in the 50's and 60's, there were two types of movie theaters. The ones owned by large businesses and ones owned independents. Almost invariably, the independents ran the older, run down theaters and the corporations ran the newer, modern ones.
>
> While there are some independents, there isn't much of a difference in size and decor.
>
> But they operated on the same premise: make enough money to pay the bills and keep the theater from going under. And that was where the corporation theaters took first prize. They had the money and the pull to get the newest shows and popular shows.
>
> Knowing that, you would think the independents would be forced to fold up.

Which wasn't the case.

Most of the independents were World War II and Korean War veterans understood what buying in bulk meant. They also knew how to draw crowds. Since they owned the concession stands and knew coca cola syrup mixed with seltzer water had a 100:1 mixture that a 12-ounce cup of ice filled with ice and 4 ounces of coke, the cost per serving was .005 per ounce, a four-ounce serving was 2 cents and the cost to the customer was 15 cents. The profit from 50 sales per show was $6.50. Popcorn that as bought in large plastic bags cost around a $2 and could generate 200 bags of popcorn for a dime produced a profit of $4.50 for 50 sales.

If you sold tickets for 25 cents and you had 50 people, you netted $12.50. The combined sales would add up to $23.50.

What if you could fill the house with 125 people and charge only 10 cents for 3 hours' worth of cartoons? You would still make $12.50 but if your concession stands sales doubled, you stood to make $22 or a total of $34.50.

In truth, the concession stand came closer to $100 profit and the $12.50 profit from the tickets was used to purchase the next week's concession stand profits. Costing $100 to run the theater every month, the theater made a profit of $4,000 just on the Saturday matinee.

The only problem with all the above, it is the way my father ran his business and to me, while that may have sounded good on paper, that wasn't even close to the money that was needed to raise a family of 6 in a town where some families made that kind of money in a day.

With that said, it usually takes a staff or crew of at least 7 people. The manager, the attractive lady selling tickets, the person who tore the tickets in half, the projection room expert, two employees working the concession stand and two floor ushers.

I think the ushers had the best job in the theater business.

First, our job was three-fold. One, when the lights were down, we would escort the patrons to their seats.

Two, when the projector room operator wanted to inform us when he was about to dim the lights and start the show.

Three, and I honestly think this was the best part of all, when kids wanted to sneak some of their friends into the theater, one of us would focus on the one or two that opened the door and the other would follow the others and wait for them to sit in the empty seats up front.

Not being the smartest kids on the block, the two that opened the door, would still be sitting near the side entrance and the ones who ran in and sat immediately in the front rows. I guess they never bothered to notice, that we scouted the empty seats before the show started and knew exactly where those empty seats were.

If the door opened on my side, I would watch the two that opened it and where they sat, and the other usher would focus on the ones that ran inside.

We would escort all of them out of the theater.

The second coolest job at the movie theater was running the projector room. You had the power to dim the lights, open and close the curtain, switch projectors, and repair the film should it break.

The job I hated was cleaning the men's and ladies' room.

But it was also part of running the theater. Something I would find to be the last thing on my mind after joining the Army.

MEMORIES OF WHAT IT USED TO BE LIKE

While these are not in as much demand in the form of a book, they still find daylight in local media.

For as far back as I can remember, when we went to Atlantic City, NJ – almost two decades before gambling casinos came to the Boardwalk – we would go there for summertime fun.

It would always be colder no matter what time of the year you came. The closer you got to the city, the saltier the air smelled.

The sky became populated with seagulls. Depending on how long the pit stops were along the way, your mind was either on hot dogs lathered with ample portions of mustard, ketchup and relish or thoughts of having your taste buds treated to things like freshly roasted peanuts, peanut brittle, popcorn, cotton candy, and saltwater taffy.

The decade of innocence – '55 to '65 – didn't have our minds on the caramel colored skin of the well-endowed beauties painting the sands like seashells. Better seen in the air by the old biplanes that would pull signs behind them with "Eat at Joe's."

The only eye candy we were looking at was being sold on the boardwalk and not under it.

The biggest problem with getting to the ocean was finding a place close enough to it to it where us kids could grab our pails, shovels, towels and large beach umbrella – which always smelled like Army-issued clothing.

You had to walk over top of the boardwalk and then down to the sands where the naked feet would be provided with an education on how glass absorbs heat. You walked much faster to the cooler, harder sand that told of the tide going out.

Once the umbrella staked our claim to a 5 x 7-foot area of sand and our towels were secured to the sand like a picture in a picture frame, we were off for our first adventure of the day.

Seashell collecting.

With an active imagination, I saw seashells as each having a story of their own. Who lived in them and died so I could tell their story. What were they protecting? What did they hide? And what marvelous stories did they tell!

Of course, the reality if it is, these shells were washed ashore because their owners either died because something bigger ate them, or they were thrown back in after commercial oyster fisherman gutted them and threw the remains back into the ocean.

Still, the ones that looked like Viking Horns and the softer ones that looked like spirals were always interesting because something inside might be hitching a ride. A hermit crabs.

You learned to leave certain things alone. Anything that looked like transparent jelly or washed ashore seaweed, for example. Both could prove quite dangerous.

The wind can blow a strange way. You barely have

enough time to build a wall for a sand castle before the sands dry out and distinctive lines are gone with the wind and become a useless adventure without closure.

By this point, my parents realize that my skin exposed to the elements is starting to become a pink red and it was time to pull the plug on the seashore.

Once everything was back in the car, we headed back up along the boardwalk for some food and refreshments. And the one place we always seemed to go to was Fralinger's Salt-water taffy.

Molasses was the original flavor. As the years passed, we were treated to chocolate, vanilla and a wide variety of flavors including green spearmint.

The boardwalk smelled a lot like someone had just paved a road. Like railroad ties. For many people, that smell was and is nauseating. For me, its musk and the smell of sea salt meant only one thing. I was in Atlantic City and on the boardwalk.

CREATIVE VENUES CAN WEAVE AN ARTICLE, TOO

This one is totally made up:

Imagine for a minute, you are walking up North Church Street. It's a cold, moonlight lit sky. You left a sink of plates and a screaming baby. It doesn't matter. This is much better than a Calgon Commercial aired in 1988.

This is even better. It's 1966.

You arrive at the train station early. As you do, 2018 fades like a rough draft screenplay not yet sure how that is going to exactly work.

The large clock against the old aging building with rusting hinges say it is 5:25. You peer down the tracks. I should be there, but it isn't.

You peer towards the east. In the fog so thin, you can't cut it with a knife, is a silhouette of a man wearing a street hat and a London Fog with the usual neck portion rolled up. He lights up his Camel with Lucky Strike matches.

All the matches.

At once.

One left out.

Saving it.

Reason, unknown.

The man died 9 years ago. Almost larger than life.

If both these thoughts didn't produce a warp in the space-time continuum.

Bogart, you think, as god is my witness.

"It's a cold night in a lonely town and the Eagles just won the Super Bowl."

"What did you just say," you ask incredibly.

"Oh, never mind, that never happened in my lifetime." Hundreds more chime in. Ghosts of Christmas Past.

"I get it!" you shout. "Hell has frozen over."

Bogart goes into character, "So, what's a pretty dame like yourself doing on this dank, dark, dusty, train station."

"Don't you think that's a little over the top?"

"Well everybody in Casablanca has problems. Yours may work out."

You are back at home. You've finished the dishes, warmed up the bottle, made sure it wasn't too hot or too cold and you stare down at. A glowing face pride with a chill of honesty. Where's the adventure the romance promised?

And you hear, "I was born when you kissed me. I died when you left me. I lived a few weeks while you loved me."

"Don't forget, 'and left in purgatory when you forgot me and took me for granted,' Bogie, never forget that line."

And as you rock your child to sleep, off in a distance on tracks of steel is passenger train heading from Camden, through town and back to Camden. That's what your mother told you happened.

A silenced horn of aged commerce no longer

capable of creating fond memories for future generation.

And yet it is there clear as day, calling your name. When it stops to pick you up and the conductor yells "All aboard," are you daring enough to ride that adventure into the unknown world that is your future?"

Trust me, life is too short to say no to a whisper of a memory that lived not long ago.

This one is not:

You could always tell the difference between the various trains that would rumble through town. The two passenger trains with a higher pitched horn sounded distinctive different that a freight train with that huskier sound horn.

I've always had an active imagination and have wondered what it would have been like during my parent's generation when trains weren't being driven by diesel engines generating electricity to power the wheels verses the sheer masculinity of the steam driven engine.

Back in the early part of the '50s the steam engine whistle could be heard of into the distance but as time went by, fewer and fewer of them were seen publicly.

On a clear, dark and quiet night, if you didn't mind the mosquitoes, you could hear the hiss of the steam locomotive and that distinctive release of steam coming from the pistons as the wheels pushed against the steel rails made especially for them to move on.

There was a large old home off to the right corner of North Stanwick Road and 3rd Street – just beyond the railroad tracks heading north which seemed out of place. Much like the steam engine, its prime and its true purpose seemed out of sync against the tapestry of the newer and younger buildings. These newer dwellings talked of city life and not farm life, of money being spent on prestige rather than the results of working the land and of social grace rather than the love for what the land could produce from the strength of labor and the sweat from the brow.

Yes, you could call it old, historic, and dying for the lack of upkeep. A big eyesore in your community and I would call it a home that spoke of a younger, golden time when the air was filled with the joy of children skipping rope, growing up and traveling in time to a far-off location where their own stories turned into golden memories of doing it their own way.

I could image steam engines as they rumbled past with hissing steam pipes, rattling windows and the distinct steam driven whistle totally distinctive of the times. You couldn't imagine the same for the newer homes which shared no such past.

Decades of the time's given experiences that can only be seen by an active imagination. Now, it is like looking at a place dying a slow but proud kind of way.

I was one of those kids who loved the scent of tar and railroad track ties. Balancing on the steel bar was something you did to pass the time. You knew the train timetables by heart. But you constantly listened for the one that wasn't.

I used to listen for the train going through from Camden and Mount Holly and then act like it was a race from Chester to Stanwick.

I always respected trains.

So, this one afternoon on Saturday, an almost familiar passenger train horn tickled my sensitive ears and my imagination.

Never heard one like that, never on a Saturday since the commuter trains don't usually on a Saturday go through town.

But the old lady who lived in that house had and she knew exactly what it was.

While that train passed, and she was waving a white handkerchief with tears rolling down her weathered face. I saw the soldiers on that train that she wasn't just waving at the soldiers heading for Vietnam in 1965.

She was waving at what her memory of those trains going to Fort Dix throughout her life there at that same exact spot for all the men of WWII and Korea. Men who would never come home alive. Men who would be mentally and physically scarred for life. Now the men on that train were heading somewhere else a place called Vietnam.

It was awe inspiring and the most amazing moment of my childhood because where she stood and why she stood there waving was just as haunting to her as it was for me watching her going back in her own world of time when they never came home to say good bye.

Very soon, in a way, I would be one of those soldiers heading for an unknown and uncertain future.

Would I come back? And in one piece? Only my own train with destiny would reveal this to me over time.

FAKE NEWS

You don't need a dictator and a regime like the crap we're putting up with today to realize what has been going on since the beginning this "great country" has been in existence. We're just more aware of the smell of manure being shelved under our noses.

Or at least some of us are.

Some folks might suggest that "Fake News" is something that Donald Trump made up ... becoming, in itself "Fake News."

Here's my definition:

Fake News is the use of any medium resource – TV, radio, magazine, newspaper, gossip or group effort – that uses its powers to put your common sense into a coma.

Cigarette smoking is good for your health. True or false?

The chemical definition: a toxic colorless or yellowish oily liquid that is the chief active constituent of tobacco. It acts as a stimulant in small doses, but in larger amounts blocks the action of autonomic nerve and skeletal muscle cells. Nicotine is also used in insecticides.

What can I conclude from this?

Well, first, I have always thought that smoking calms me down. Guess I was wrong about that.

Also, excuse me, but I haven't gone to medical school, so what is an autonomic nervous system?

The clinical definition: The autonomic nervous system is a control system that acts largely unconsciously and regulates bodily functions such as the heart rate, digestion, respiratory rate, papillary response, urination, and sexual arousal.

Okay, so now I can conclude nothing because, again, another fancy word has been thrown at me: constituent. What does that mean?

Well, aside from the fact that it means I'm uneducated, it means that it is in the tobacco.

The bottom line is cigarette smoking is bad for your health. I get it. What I don't get is the game that is being played on the amount of fake tobacco that is in the new cigarettes and how much nicotine is being chemically added to the non-tobacco fillers. For example, if I go to the local convenience store and purchase an $8 pack of my Kool 100s, they are packed so loosely that when I do pack them, they are about if a King. On the other hand, if I go to the store where the Indian Reservation sells them for $6, they are packed tight.

You would think from that, I'm getting a bargain. Not true. I find myself wheezing more, coughing more and I must smoke more often. In fact, for the past several years, perhaps because I've been around many people who have been using smokeless cigarettes, I've noticed the smell of nicotine to be as strong if not stronger in cigarettes. I can also taste it on my lips.

Bottom line, regardless of whether you believe me or not, I must quit smoking. Not because of hype but because breathing in carbon monoxide isn't a healthy ticket to living longer.

But if I told you a lie and said smoking it good for

you, you're not going to believe me. But what if 100 or more people commented that they 100% agree?

Truth is, if you say something often enough and it is seen by hundreds of people as "true," that is most likely a form of fake news.

Especially, if the American Press whose position in life was impeccable, informative and the consciousness of the American People.

Truth is, if someone doesn't agree, and his or her comments are removed, it's propaganda.

Well, as we all know, Fox News is living proof that a one-sided republican News organization without a counter news system in place will not and cannot present information that offers anything but a propaganda. Most Americans with an IQ past 100 can see this for what it is. 100% fake news.

At the same level of journalistic jungle book chest beating mentality as the *Star* or *Enquirer*. But you could try to say your mind with these through editorials. They just won't get published.

The problem is, web based social mediums do not enable freedom of speech at all. In fact, it is the only communicative medium that has gone out of its way to assure top feeders can say anything they want to say to anyone they want to say it to. That's fake news.

If I can't even get the Washington Post or the Chicago Tribune, for example, to point out a glaring truth about the so called "Homeless man" story, for example, then only people with money able to purchase time in the American Press news system and democracy has died.

The image above shows, clearly, a man and a

woman working the corner where the "homeless man" story claims to have gotten started. And I do mean exact position. Note the male siting down and hiding from the view of the traffic coming off I-95. He only gets up when there is a long line of traffic coming from the south. It is normally a rarity to see a female panhandler. But a more important point is, the two knew how to work the corner. And that doesn't happen if you haven't been doing this for some time.

Unfortunately, TV has been more focused on the rich rather than providing a balanced local social news system that provides support for all people in their community. When I was working for "Pastor Jack" at the Lake Charles Southern Baptist Homeless Shelter for Men back in 1990 I would clean up and handle the men coming through, so I could stay there.

Most of the men were professional street people. Clean, smart, and basically on the street because they wanted to, or they just fell on some hard times. The fabulous Thunderbirds lead singer was set to do a show a few blocks away.

So, this young man comes walking in, I do the paperwork processing, take no care to notice much of a difference in him than anyone else coming through. Until he signed his name. I've been around a few celebrities in my life and the way he signed his name looked like an autograph.

I instantly looked up and studied his face. My eyes read a sadness and a confidence in that face.

His name was Jimmie Ray Vaughan. I didn't have to know anything about him. I didn't. Nor did I know Stevie Ray Vaughan had just got killed. All I knew was this man wasn't the type that would have expected to visit a homeless shelter. I said, "I'm betting you play a mean guitar."

That got him to smile.

So, when it came time for Pastor Jack to pull out his guitar and do his usual ritual of playing a Southern Baptist themed song for all of us, I said, "Pastor Jack, you really, really, really need to give this man here your guitar."

The man played it like heaven just dropped in for a visit.

So, I decided that another way to lighten up his spirits and help put him back into the saddle so to speak was to take him over to KPLC TV in Lake Charles, LA. I talked to Cynthia Arceneaux and told her about him. Cause you're wondering, despite my homeless situation, I had built a rapport with the local press and Cynthia agreed to talk to him.

Well, that didn't exactly turn out the way I wanted it to. Not because I did anything, but because I could clearly see that Jimmy Ray Vaughan was blowing them off.

Anyway, after we got outside, I said, "Jimmy, why didn't you tell them the truth? Why did you blow them off?"

He said, "Because they weren't believing a thing I said."

A little reflection and I had to agree. They weren't seeing the man; they were seeing a bum off the streets.

I never saw Jimmy Ray Vaughan again. But I'm betting Cynthia Arceneaux had wished she had done this famous guitar player's story.

The point: If you can't convince your local TV station with a story of a lifetime, what are the chances the average Joe's story is ever going to grab their attention?

With that said, let's move on. Imagine, for a moment that an article comes out in a highly visible publication that totally scares the hell out of everyone. It was a clear-cut statement of fact that could be replicated repeatedly with the user of the product dead quicker than a true natural death. Of course, sales dropped like a helium-inflated lead balloon.

I'm sure you've figured out what the product was. Together, tobacco companies and the PR firm created and funded an organization called the Tobacco Industry Research Committee to produce results and opinions that contradicted the view that smoking kills.

Therefore, the tobacco companies haven't died as fast as its cancer victims.

So, if only one publication proves a fatal fact, all it takes is someone to come along with just as much clout to make just as visible claims to the contrary. This was the birth and the best example of "fake news."

When someone damns an obvious villain – for example, the cause and effect of global warming, all it takes is to have an opposing interest with more money and power to create a similar organization like the Tobacco Industry Research Committee, to come along and counter it with "fake news."

You can pretty much count on things like the FCC, FDA to be massive cover up fronts for big businesses in America.

The question which raises its ugly head is, why in the world can't we see fake news for what it is? And I harbor the belief that the primary reason why is because we were born and programmed to believe in authority figures. After all, our parents did. Parents are infallible, right?

The other more reasonable answer may just be as simple as this. The family does things a certain way because it just works for them. And when a child asks, the parents say, "Well that's the way we've done things and it has always worked in the past."

But when the child becomes an adult and a parent and that family tradition of doing things in the past gets challenged, the answer played like a tape recording not only becomes irrelevant, it sounds corny and trite.

So, when the parent asks the older parent again, the response is, "Well, darling, we just told you that to get you off our backs."

In other words, some agreements at the time they were made were based on a need to take affirmative action. Past that point they become institutionalized until such time those same agreements are no longer true and need to be re-evaluated and dropped or adjusted to address a similar issue with a difference purpose.

Ever since the time that President Donald Trump labeled anything he didn't care or want to hear from the press as "Fake News," I've been biting at the bit to write an article on what I know is money driven and money making promotional advertorials.

But the more I thought about it, the more I realized this 1st Amendment cancer has been plaguing free press from as far back as I dare to remember.

In fact, "Fake News" is nothing more than a reflection of just how gullible and out of touch the American public has become. It isn't the responsibility of the press to deliver accurate and timely information when the hand that would feed that delivery would rather hear about the President's wife's wardrobe over the fact that people are dying in Puerto Rico as a direct result of hurricane damage.

Unlike the times when Shepard Smith was down in New Orleans and calling on the government to get fresh water to people who had none, it was painfully apparent that our response to local disasters can address real time issues

SOME TRICKS AND TIPS

As I pointed out previously, there are a variety of ways you can mix and match to create some very interesting articles.

One of these is Faction. Don't mix Faction up with Advertorials.

Faction is the art of taking non-fiction and adding some drama to it to make the story come alive.

Fiction uses a concept core to all genres you will ever learn to love. An event must happen to the main hero or heroine that causes him or her to have to do something he or she wasn't prepared to do.

The something will always point to a weakness in the hero's or heroin's' character and he or she must overcome it to survive. This creates tension.

My first article in *EurArmy Magazine* involved a non-fiction situation where our AH-1Q Model Cobras were supposed to fire Tube Launched, Optically Tracked, Wire Guided – TOW missiles down range.

Since the TOW missiles had to be fired at targets that could be seen by the front seat gunner.

Unfortunately, the combination of snow and fog wasn't making it easy to meet the scheduled training times. We were losing the window of opportunity. Since we have no control of the weather, this was an opportune time to add the tension fiction writing would bring to the article.

Seemingly unaffected by gravity, snow drops

slowly and softly to the ground.

But you could tell much about how much was coming down with a fog so thick you could cut it with a knife.

Blowing the fog around occasionally, it would give you a peek at the hunting, silent birds of prey rising above the ground like dark metal warriors.

The smell of breakfast coffee and freshly cooked bacon fill the air as high pitched – banshees sounding – generators supply electricity and noise for the solders to follow between the tenets, the field mess hall and the Tactical Operation Center.

The door opens, and a hand passes the guard a steamy cup or enthusiasm. The solider thanks the officer for a cup of redemption.

"We're going to go hot today, sir. I can feel it in my bones."

"I certainly hope so," says Major Esmay, the OIC of the TOC for the 3rd Combat Aviation Battalion, 3rd Infantry Division while puffing on his pipe, "we've already had our fair share of disappointment."

Advertorials on the other hand are nothing more than a cold sale method so archaic with respect to selling you on a product, you can literally template what is said and how it is said.

The core concept: Before you met me, you didn't realize how much value and importance the product or service is to you and your life. When I'm finished educating and informing you on the key reasons why my products or services are important to you, you will buy these products and services because you now know you just can't live without them.

But these tactics just don't stop at cold selling.

Also, imagine, for a moment that an article comes out in a highly visible publication that totally scares the hell out of everyone. It was a clear-cut statement of fact that could be replicated repeatedly with the user of the product dead.

I'm sure you've figured out what the product was. Together, tobacco companies and the PR firm created and funded an organization called the Tobacco Industry Research Committee to produce results and opinions that contradicted the view that smoking kills.

Therefore, the tobacco companies haven't died as fast as its cancer victims.

So, if only one publication proves a fatal fact, all it takes is someone to come along with just as much clout to make just as visible claims to the contrary.

This was where "fake news" got its start. When someone damns an obvious villain – for example, the cause and effect of global warming, all it takes is to have an opposing interest with more money and power to create a similar organization like the Tobacco Industry Research Committee, to come along and counter it with "fake news."

By the way, "fake news" won the presidency for Donald Trump. It's amazing just how quickly he fired the focus from himself to the press. Millions heard the talks and millions voted for him over Hillary Clinton. For exactly that reason.

Funny thing about it is, those who voted for him are losing jobs left and right. And the rich got a tax break the size equal to a retirement check for 20,000,000 Americans who will never have a retirement because the companies they own don't have a retirement system in place.

That's what most of mine have done over the years. Fact is, seems like everybody and his or her brother, aunt, uncle, step mom, stepfather and I Robot have the talent to write. And they all make promises that you can make $1,000 by just following this or that.

Let's look at the following.

As a result, the U.S. government, rather than provide statistical proof, attempted to guide its population to good health. Unfortunately, this "guidance" was based partly on nonexistent science and partly on faulty science. And it ignored humanity's long history of a diet that for several million years was based on hunting and gathering - which likely included high amounts of fat and animal products - and replaced it with one that aimed to reduce this fat consumption to less than 10%.

What do you see?

I see a good propagandist taking one to know one and throwing stones at a glass house before someone throws a stone at his.

Let's distill this down to one line.

The U.S. government guidelines on fat consumption should be less than 10%.

Okay, so why all the fluff? The author is commanding attention as the authorized tactician seeing the battlefield from above the game. Anytime someone does this, they program in what I call "key sleepers."

Which also means I am also playing on your perceptions rather than just the facts:

as a result
rather than
attempted to
unfortunately
partly on
it ignored
for
based on
which likely
high amounts
replaced it
with one
that aimed
to reduce
this fat
to less than

What's the main premise?

While the government's new diet is aimed to reduce the fat consumption to 10%, the government is ignoring humanity's long history of a diet that for several million years was based on hunting and gathering - which likely included high amounts of fat and animal products.

Hey, I didn't write this, someone else did. And this is what a real journalist does to ether create real "fake news" or create professional class reporting.

Okay so are we really talking about a diet here or well-balanced meals. These are two different concepts.

I want to verify the fat consumption limit the government has recommended. What's the link to that website.

You mention that our hunter-gatherers most likely ate high amounts of fat and animal products. It is too weak of an argument unless you believe the notion that several million years provides credibility. If you can't prove this, drop it.

Believe me, I'm my own worst enemy when it comes to things like this.

Rule #1: No one likes to be preached to. Suppose I should take some of that medicine myself.

Rule #2: Making a person laugh or feel good about themselves is a big is a good way to break the ice.

Rule #3: Leave no stone unturned. Create a list of questions that must be answered before you write the paragraph.

Rule #4: Never believe a stranger's word at face value. You need to verify anyone you quote as a viable source.

There some tricks along the way that will make it much easier to take the bitter with the sweet. Well, to be honest with you, I can't promise you anything.

No one can.

And honestly, I'm lousy at sugarcoating freelance writing as being a ten-year reunion of published work.

It's been more like 30, but who's counting.

The fact is, if you are still here reading this, you're beginning to like me and my writing style and not looking for credentials, but the voice of experience. And let's face it, you aren't here looking for a Tony Robbins, you're looking for key words that jump off the page and grab your interest.

I am also a realist and I don't believe you should be

suckered into a book that uses flashy numbers to entice you into purchasing a book. So, let me be clear. I am not interested in you buying this book, I am interested in helping you become a published writer.

Sure, I can highlight some very successful writers, publishers and TV show producers that I've had the pleasure of knowing and working with, does that make you a better writer or professional freelancer?

No.

In fact, when it comes down to it, telling you anything about my past is just another way of trying to sell you this book. And I don't believe you are here for that.

But I am about to whet your appetite with respect to what I have planned. So, here goes.

WRITING IS THE ABILITY TO TAKE IDEAS, GATHER FACTS AND TURN THAT INTO SOMETHING THAT HELPS THE READER GET A WARM AND FUZZY FEELING ALL OVER

Let's say you want to write for Bicycling Magazine. You see that they accept articles that enrich and embrace the bicycle lifestyle as a means of travel and recreation.

So, the questions you want to ask are:

- What is the length of the article they accept?
- Do images enhance the chances the story will be accepted?
- Has a similar article been published recently?
- Are there enough interesting facts to make it worth reading?

The typical writer spends more time working on selling faction, fiction, non-fiction and photo features than on improving their writing skills. No one, not even myself, can improve their writing if they are measuring their writing against time, word count and the amount of checks being issued.

Furthermore, people who tell you to write about what you know must be practicing being a politician.

Tell you what you want to hear and, at the same time, know it is a lie.

Truth is, almost 90% of all rejection slips added to returned manuscripts happen when your write what you know.

A simple question will help to align the concept: Are you the only human being on the planet?

Sounds silly. You know you aren't.

But, try to convince fisherman who's reading a Bass Magazine that wearing a straw hat and fishing from a bamboo raft enhances catching large-mouth Bass, unless your Huckleberry Finn, is probably going to get instant rejection. Even if you were Mark Twain.

It isn't what you know that sells your work, it's what the reader wants to know about the subject.

Despite what you might read from a Facebook group, the fact is, communications are a two-way street. You cannot communicate your writing if what you write is your way of thinking and not your reader's way of thinking.

So, sensitivity to what the reader wants to know and written in a logic pattern designed to take them from beginning to end is the best approach to sell the article.

HAVE CAMERA, WILL TRAVEL

There used to be a TV series called the *Wild, Wild West*. Something of a *Have Gun, Will Travel* wannabe. Will Smith tried to revive it a few decades back; it died a horrible death. Kind of like my mad attempts to convince my wife that travel writing, and photography can be a lucrative.

The truth is, it is. However, it is not as lucrative as one would hope considering there are literally hundreds of thousands of various outlets for your work. You just must sift through all the dirt and find the gold others have left behind.

Or, just go to places where there is gold but harder to find and get to.

Okay, so let's drop the cuteness and talk about the cold hard facts.

A lot of well off husband and wife teams make a ton of money from travel writing and photography because they know how to work the interstate highway system.

Add that to the fact that every person with a digital camera or cell phone camera can take images of people, places and things along the major highways and cities with the result a flooded market with no profitable option in sight.

Well, fortunately, there are still tons of people, places and things that can make you money; you just must go find them. Let me give you an example of where not to go in Arizona:

- Grand Canyon
- Sedona
- Prescott
- Phoenix
- Usury Park
- Lost Dutchman State Park
- Renaissance Festival
- Boyce Thompson Arboretum
- Tucson
- Old Tucson Stage Set
- Sonora Desert Museum
- Pima Air Museum
- Sierra Vista
- Davis Monthan Air Force Base
- Fort Huachuca
- Kirchner Caverns
- Benson
- Boot Hill
- Tombstone
- Wilcox
- Flagstaff
- Meteor Creator
- Biosphere
- Red Mountain Park
- Bisbee
- Douglas
- Nogales
- Goldfield Mining Camp

- Yuma
- Any other place I missed that popular with the tourists.

In other words, pretty much the entire state.

Which begs, why am I here?

I am here because the true treasures of these places aren't on the maps. It is at the location and it's the people, plants, animals and the rich history that them come alive for readers.

So, the trick is to look for an interesting angle that makes the same location feel different to the readers.

Still not convinced?

When I was in the military, public affairs journalist would only cover a specific unit once a year. I made them think differently. Every unit has tons of Human Interest stories. Interesting characters both in the service and out of the service.

Well, the same thing goes for every place on me don't go list. Including ghost towns like Fairbank and Charleston. Here are some ideas off the top of my head:

- The other side of Charleston time has forgotten about.
- The role Fairbank played as a railroad hub.
- Fort Huachuca. The military base where the past, present and future
- Army Intelligence
- Captain Neuman MD
- Is Serra Vista a great place to retire?
- Bisbee's torrid past
- Three great places in Bisbee to stay

- Bisbee Bed and Breakfast – a quaint old school conversion worth staying for a night
- Tombstone famous gunfight wasn't done at the OK Corral.
- How the press battled the bad guys with black ink
- Johnny Ringo isn't buried at Boot Hill
- San Pedro River – A river with an attitude problem
- The history of Father Pedro
- Kirchner Caverns – more there than what meets the eye
- The Stage Set Annex few know exists
- Marie Osmond was here; at least, that's what it says
- Southern Pacific's Diesel engine graveyard
- The Triple T Truck stop restaurant has the best food ever
- The world of snakes, spiders and badass looking scorpions
- The Pima Air Museum – too cold and too old for the price of admission
- Tucson – More bookstores than strip clubs
- Tucson – The best display of summer curves getting tanned in the sun
- Tucson – Tore down my first apartment and turned it into a retirement home
- Tucson – 12 best spots to take images of trains
- Tucson – 12 best spots to take images of Air Force planes

- Tucson – 12 best spots to take images of commercial and private planes
- Old Tucson – A look back to when the west was lost.
- Sonora Desert Museum – Some new displays worth revisiting
- Biosphere – from the outside looking in.

Okay, so here's the idea. You want to make money as you travel from place to place. Sometimes making money comes in the form of making your work visible to the entire world. And the amount of views your images get will tell you a lot about their uniqueness.

That's why the first place I go with my images to Google Maps. It's free and your images will get seen. But there is another reason why Google Maps can help you increases your chances to land a story with your images to a publication.

Included with every location where your images are being viewed by others is also a review of the place. And you can get a good feel for what people like and don't like about the location.

This information is invaluable for a variety of reasons. The best being the reviews have done a lot of fact-finding legwork for you. The second best is the fact that the reviews will also tell you a lot about the attitude of the owner or staff towards tourists. The third best is you may be good with a camera and get the images you want but you may not be able to return to the location to write the article or vice versa. Other local guides could help you complete the requirements.

Another opportunity you may want to consider is

the Groupon Partner Network.

One of my daughters decided to take a flying lesson. It was a great experience for her. But it could also have been a moment when a write up on Groupon coupled with a touch of business savvy could move the experience towards a tidy profit of 10% for every purchase of a Groupon product or service.

Suppose, for example you linked yourself to 52 products and the average referral netted you 10% and that percent was going against products or services charging $100. If your referrals hit 1000, your profit for your efforts is going to net you $520,000.

IT'S YOUR CAREER, NOT MINE

Up until now, I've been short on words. I've been saving the last 6 to 10 topic areas because I wanted to get my ideas out.

Most you who have gotten to this point in this book are probably wondering why there wasn't a lot more of me reflecting on my career.

Well, to be honest with you, it is complicated.

It was always complicated and will always be complicated.

Why? Because, technically, my last name is Steen and not Edwards. A Copenhagen ancestor by the name of Edward Steen came to this country and decided he should be called Steen Edwards.

Edward Steen married a Mary Ann Dare whose family changed their name from Dyer to Dare. Boston has a statue of a Mary Dyer. She was hanged there for her religious beliefs and for her damn stubbornness.

Up until my Dad's father died the family would continue the tradition of going there once a year to honor the woman who refused to back down.

Even though Steen Edwards named one of his son's Adolph E. Steen. Adolph Eugene Steen had a son from his second marriage named Eugene Richard Edwards and I am Richard T. Edwards.

I am fourth generation of the Steen family here in the United States. And after seeing Norway up close and personally I want to ring Edward Steen's neck. There were only three Steens of stature born in the 1800s. Adolph Steen, Edward Steen and Johannes Steen and there's eight and a half years between all three. 1810, 1816 and 1827, respectively.

I inherited their soup of genetic genius. With a twist of Dyslexia thrown in for good measure.

There is a reason why I devoured children's books when I was young.

In Langland, Denmark, the tie between Copenhagen and Norway apparently includes a man by the name of Hans Christen Anderson who spent time in Langland, too. I loved the way the words flowed. Short, sweet and to the point.

But I can have my moments when an acquaintance of mine is being bugged by his beloved followers – some 50,000 – and instead of saying, guys, leave the Pulitzer Prizewinner alone, he needs silence to think, I said:

> Whisper quietly oh gentle fold of o be ones. Whilst his gray matter of highly organized thoughts flow like a spring against the dark side of drought and doubt, we must silence our ourselves until the work is mastered and we wonder in amazement how the blood of living breathing tissue set us upon a path of ink laced chosen words in spell binding order. Quenching our desire to be amazed.

Who the hell writes like that?

I do, but he's too often down along the Strawbridge Lake, in Moorestown, NJ, acting like Tom Sawyer under an old weeping willow tree. Catching Sun Fish with ten-pound-test catgut and some number 6 hooks, weights, a bobber and night crawler worms dug out from the back yard. Shooing away pesky summertime Mosquitoes.

My escape from Alcatraz.

But I was a total mess. Taking everything literally, I would "take up the cross." A rather comical visual when you think of about it. A kid carrying a homemade cross around the backyard. I did my best to be in character.

Or literally didn't believe anything anyone said. When I told my mother, I could read up and down and left and right and upside down and wanted to read for right to left otherwise I didn't understand a thing, I was "lazy." So, I took her literally.

"Hello, my name is lazy and lazy is my name.

In 1966, this "lazy" tenth grader was required to take the PSAT tests and scored in the top 3% of the country.

As for writing, I'm a natural when I want to be. Right now, isn't one of them. My High School English teacher would read my writing to the class and remark how great it was. So, she wrote in my yearbook, if I could only learn how to spell, I would be a great writer.

In other words, they are now assigned to the units and not to a division public affair. They are out in the field where they should be. And what this does is have a central public affairs coordinator who screens out unwanted press from going directly these journalists.

Just the way I used to do it.

I had my images stocked by Black Star Publishing and my images were published throughout the world.

Technically, I'm the most published unofficial writer and photographer in the history of the US Army.

My makeup was on stage with Jefferson Starship.

I've worked as a contributing editor for Opportunity and Income Plus. One of his covers was a picture of mine and one of the features is directly responsible for Riverboat Gambling in Lake Charles, LA.

I've had nice, decent art images published by Bruce Helford when he was the editor for the Bits and Pieces Section of Hustler Magazine. He also became the producer of Anger Management and the Drew Carey Show.

Two images of mine are part of a 135 photographers collection Shirrel Rhoades donated to the Savannah College of Arts and Design. The collection in which Shirrel Rhoades said were 135 lensmen who'd had a significant impact of the history of photography.

Before I went to Microsoft in 1996, I had 6 magazine covers and hundreds of images published throughout the world.

I have been working either for Microsoft or supporting Microsoft products until last October. At that point, I decided it was time to retire and start getting back into the saddle of writing and photography.

And since I've had experience writer on almost all the playing fields you will be starting your writing career using, I figured the best place to start would be helping you with a book like this.

What I'm discovering is, while the methods and techniques used in this book so far and tried, true and are timeless, the way you get them published has become dramatically different and more difficult than I ever had to deal with.

You're going to have to find traction in a world where information once inaccessible is no accessible and free. Where patience is impatient and where tolerance for spelling and grammatical errors is now unacceptable.

Let me put it to you a different way. It you've ever played tennis, you know that you start off as a C player. At this level, you're barely able to volley, much less control where the ball goes or understand the strategies behind the game. A player refuses to play with you because you stink at the game.

Eventually, your hand and eye coordination improve, your ability to serve also improves and you get to the point where you can do all sorts of cool stuff like put spin on the ball and drive the opponent bunkers with fast aces and cool spins.

I broke a Head racquet yoke returning a AAA player's volley and bought a Spalding Speedshaft to replace it. None of my children knows what that means, but if you are reading this and you've played tennis, you can share my humor when one without any instruction wanted me to "volley" with them thinking they were going to beat me.

Well that's kind of where you are now. You want to beat me at my game. Honorable and formidable of you but there is a lot of learning to be done. And I've hoped I've helped so far. But you're in the C category and, it's my turn to teach you a thing or two so you can become an A player.

TAKING A STEP BACKWARDS

Before we go any further, let's take a step backwards and take a swing at some of the basic facts about some core business concepts. First you need to get a business license – your tennis racquet – and run your own business through your house. Done correctly, a designated room or area for your business is a tax write off. So, will any of the equipment you use, the gas you spend and the wear and tear on your car.

That's the first step. The second step is to realize that the Army has a pretty good bead on how exactly your work should be thought through and organized.

- Research, prepare and disseminate news releases, articles, web-based material and photographs on Army personnel and activities
- Gather information for military news programs and publications within your unit and around the Army
- Develop ideas for news articles
- Arrange and conduct interviews
- Write news releases, feature articles and editorials
- Conduct media training

Let me rewrite this:

- Research, create, edit and send news releases, articles, web-based material and photographs on people, places and things local, state, regional, country and world news outlets would be interested in using.

- Gather information for TV, radio, magazines and newspapers at the local, state, regional, country and world news outlets would be interested in using.
- Develop ideas for news articles
- Arrange and conduct interviews
- Educate and inform your local community on the value and importance your products and services have on the local community.

The last one is your tennis court. The place where you call the shots and you establish your own territory.

So then, this begs, are you the only one on the court? In fact, how many jobs in the world of freelance writing are in your area?

Just go to Google and type in freelance writers in Redmond, WA. Or whereever. Who knows, might be your first job as a freelancer.

But what exactly does educate and inform your local community on the value and importance your products and services have on the local community mean? It means you're selling, by example, what your work means to the community.

Why do you want to do this?

Because you're wanting to do three things:

1. Make yourself known in the community as a person focused on promoting the town.
2. Enable your presence to be accepted by your community.

3. Display your willingness to become a team player

HOW THIS IS DONE

There was a lady the other day who asked the group how she could anchor a spot in a local bookstore and I provided her with the following ideas:

The first thing you want to do is think of yourself as a person who has never been to this bookstore.

- Is there ample parking?
- Are the spaces for RV and recreational vehicles?
- During times when Christmas shopping is at its peak, are these spaces also used by other businesses?

The second thing you want to look for is the street corner or as you open the door books for sale.

- What is the quality of the books?
- Is there a diversified mix of books available?
- Did any of them catch your eye?

The third thing you want to look at the way the store is laid out.

- Is there a coffee shop?
- Is how much space is allocated for newspapers and magazine?
- Is this a multi-level or single level store?
- Is the first thing you see a book reader?
- Is there a legend on how the bookstore is laid out?
- How much area in the front of the area is allocated for oversized books?

- Where the cashier stations are located, is there space for layaway's and ordered books?
- Is there a reading room area just for children?
- Is there an area for chilling out?
- Are there computer stations for book searching?
- How cordial are the floor people?
- How quickly are you able to find a book and go through the cashier stations and back to your car?

The Fourth thing you want to do is look for ways you can enhance the environment and attract new business to the store.

- Do you speak more than one language?
- Do you like reading to children?
- Do you like making books come alive for adults?
- Is there a section of books you could do reviews on?
- What books interest you the most?
- What's your favorite coffee drink?
- What kinds of newspapers are available?
- What kinds of magazines are available?
- Are you into computers and various programming languages?
- Are you into writing?
- Are you into photography?
- Are you going to college?

You're probably wondering what the point to all of this was. Simple, marry up what you know with what is available to you to ether learn more or enrich other's experiences with books is a great way to provide yourself with visibility and help the book store to showcase how books improve the quality of life and make life itself much more enjoyable.

But this is just one business. Imagine for a moment that you have hundreds of businesses in your area that would not only love to get some free publicity by would also enable you to work interactively with their business.

Think about it for a minute, you could profile hundreds of different business for years on end and never talk to all the owners or know all the stores that will help you make money in more ways you can imagine.

The key is to talk to the managers and owners and see if they have any copies of trade publications that he or she has laying around that he or she doesn't want. Why would you want to do this?

That owner or manager will also tell you what he or she would like to see in these business publications and, if you ask, might be interested, should the publication use business profiles, in you doing one on them.

I really can't emphasize this enough. The best way to make money from businesses is through commercial and trade publications you acquire from these businesses. But you must know the publication uses business profiles and the owners are willing to talk to you once you have approval to profile the business from the publication.

Furthermore, contacting commercial and trade

publications, getting told no from one publication doesn't mean another will say the same.

Same thing goes with the businesses you contact. Not every business owner wants his or her business profiled. You may find a similar business in town or in another town close by that will say yes.

Remember, what you're doing is highly speculative. One store may not want to share their trade publications with you. Another store might but doesn't want the publicity. But the third store might want both commercial and trade publication publicity.

I would love to say there is a ton of money to be made here. The truth is, you can make more than you think but it also better that you start with baby steps first.

SEXY MEMORIES

I am the first to admit that I love sexy. And I can be quite graphic. This is just a fun innuendo.

My family went through a lot of cars over the years. When my dad bought one, it was always a bomb. For some reason, he would always get suckered into buying one that was either on its last legs or such an eye sore, it needed to be repaired just to get to the junkyard.

Well, I guess he finally got tired on getting pistol whipped by my mother and he got a 1962 Chevy Impala. In 1967.

It was one of those four wheels, four doors with a 283 three-speed transmission and push-button radios you had to hit every one in a while to make it work.

There were only two radio stations us kids were interested in back in the '60s. WIBG – A/K/A wibbage – and WFIL – A/K/A wiffle. The two stations were opposites on the AM band. WFIL was 520 and WIBG was 990.

Only reason why I remember any of the radio DJs was because a dial-nower. Okay, I made that up, but it is the best way to describe people who listen to a radio station because they want to win something. And, pretty much he was an addict. Which sparked his natural desire to gamble.

But that's not important. The fact is, I knew the DJ names: George Michael, Jim Nettleton, Long John Wade, and Donald T. Rose.

I think I met them all, too. Donald T. Rose I wanted to use for a dance. But his fee cut too much into the profit line, so I dropped it.

As far as I was concerned, the car had three purposes in life. Get me to work, get me to the mall and get me out on dates.

Problem with the car was, it wasn't a muscle car and it didn't sound "bad." It was a whale and as far as I was concerned, a slug.

It had plastic seat covers. The kind, that in the dead of winter you could have started the car up with the static electricity you built up

Imaging you and your girlfriend in heat. You get naked, open the doors and eagerly jump into the back seat.

Last thing on your mind, indeed, the last thing that might ever be on your mind and FORGET about the fact that when your butts on top of a wool blanket sliding across the plastic produces enough static electricity to fry your brains, light up New York City or split atoms.

I mean, really, you didn't have to have an orgasm, you just did.

"Wow, that was fantastic."

"Your hair is standing up."

"Smoke is coming out of your ears."

"Can we try that again?"

"No."

I think I just created a new fad. Headlines: A shocking new way of birth control.

Okay, enough of the shock treatment.

HOW TO MAKE YOUR CAR SOUND BAD WHEN IT'S A WHIMP

Okay, things like 3/4 in racing cams, four-barrel carbs, and glass pack exhaust systems, boring out the engine and putting in larger pistons and rings would be a total waste of time and money.

The easiest way to make your car sound like a bad ass was to take off the black air filter cover. The effect made the engine sound like a very large masculine sounding vacuum cleaner. Picked up a couple more horses out of it, too.

Anyway, the effect turned heads and made people wonder what was under the hood. Which was nothing.

So, one day, after finishing a class at RCA Institute of Electronics, with everyone burning rubber, I decided to do the same. So, I revved up the engine and popped the clutch.

One slight problem. I forgot the parking break. BAM went the transmission and my pride. I wimped it out of the parking lot in 3rd gear.

"Mom"

"Yes, Richard."

"I think there's something wrong with the car. It won't go into 1st or 2nd anymore."

"Can you fix it?"

"Sure!"

"Well, you have the money. Fix it."

Which I did. Cost me $25 to buy a new transmission and

$50 to watch a mechanic remove and replace it in less than 30 minutes.

At McDonalds in Lenola, NJ, at the corner of Lenola Rd and W. Camden Ave, the boys were once again showing off their muscle cars. And, again, I forgot to release the parking break.

"Mom"

"Yes, Richard."

"I think I bought a bad transmission. It won't go into 1st or 2nd anymore."

"You know what to do."

I put that one in myself. And the car worked fine until I went into the service.

THE RACE I LOST BUT WON

I was pretty good at coming off the intersections and getting the car up to 60 in short order. Unfortunately, the car just didn't have the power to do much else.

There used to be light on 38 just before you got to the overpass at the Cherry Hill Mall, where a Pontiac 442 pulled up beside me. I revved, he revved, and I concentrated on the red light turning green.

As soon as I did, I saw the cop coming on the off ramp and heading onto 38. I got to 60 and maintained the speed the speed limit. The 442, of course, at this point blew the doors off my 62 Chevy and in less than 30 seconds, the cop had his lights on pulling him over.

His wife was yelling at him as I passed by and he looked at me with one of those looks that says it all, "If I find you, I'm going to kill you."

I stopped trying to be a Billy bad ass with a car that was needed by the family to survive.

Still, it was a fun car to drive.

REVISIONS

Have you ever thought about what you could add to your normal 1500 to 3000-word features that you write for commercial publications?

(Hold up, wait, the sentence just doesn't feel right, let me rewrite it.)

Reflecting on your published work, have you ever thought about improving it? And if you did, do you think it would have any effect on the next submission?

(Now, I feel much better about where this is going and what the real article is about. We can now rejoin the article's train of thought.)

The truth is, while you can sell Eskimos ice cubes, your approach to getting them to use them for their cold drinks is a different story all together.

But first, let's summarize, where you were and how you got here.

1. You connected to the magazine and they returned to you a listing of the articles they want to use in upcoming issues, provided you with a sample copy and writers guidelines.

2. You came up with an idea, summarized the content and pitched the idea to them.

3.They gave you an "on spec" approval and you wrote the article.

4. You then had to wait a couple of weeks to be told it was accepted for publication or it wasn't.

5. You get an acceptance letter and sign all the

forms.

6. You send a thank you letter with your returned documents along with another article idea and summary just like you did before.

7. This time, while the editor likes your idea, he or she sends you a rejection slip and asks for you to no longer submit articles to him or her.

So, why did this happen? In one word, Voice. And believe me, I have heard this repeatedly, "You impress editors and their readership when ideas and thoughts are in the pattern both want to hear and can relate to."

It truly becomes music to their ears.

It all boils down to word choice, the correct use of gerunds, prepositional phrases and smooth transitions.

A good friend of mine by the name of John Michael Coleman who was the editor for *EurArmy Magazine* said something like this. "Tell them what you're going to say, say it; then tell them what you've said."

And if you think that is totally confusing, imagine a wet behind the ears journalist who is dyslexic trying to figure out what the heck he meant to get an article approved for publication in less than 3 days was going through.

To this day, consciously, I'm still not sure I got it. But it was what my subconscious heard. And took the ball and ran with it.

I wrote 30 articles and saw 27 go into print in *EurArmy Magazine* and the other 3 went into *Soldiers Magazine.*

In the civilian world it is like getting published in *Time* Magazine and *Life* Magazine.

With that said, let's get back on track and focus on vice, temp and word choice.

If your audience has a 9th grade education, you don't use cognizant, you use aware of. If your audience is reading the publication as a means of escaping you don't remind them of the better half with a baseball bat swing over the reader's head about to wallop him for not taking out the trash.

And then, if you really want a rejection slip, try writing your prose like this for an IT consultant.

You put the right thingy into the left thingy and flip a switch with a fire extinguisher in your hand.

"Hello, Microsoft. My Windows done died."

I'm grabbing some coffee trying to calm down the laughter.

The truth is, you must read the content in the magazine to understand what is required of you. So, while the subject and the title might attract an acceptance, getting more than one story published means you wrote the article the way the reader expects it to be written.

And believe me, I can tell when an article is generically written to be used for other publications just by its design and the way it was written.

Now, let's finish this off with some spit and polish. I was well known for the topic hook, the supportive sentence and the one-line transition.

The clearer you pave the way to your conclusion, the better your writing becomes.

Let me show you a run-on sentence and how short bursts make it flashy and easier to read:

If you are like me, chances are good that you find great pleasure, satisfaction, and pride of ownership in that brand-new car you spend lots of time cleaning and polishing like a gem in the rough. But one scratch, one dent and the honeymoon is over.

Geeze, and to think I used to write this way! Yuck!

So, you have a brand-new car. You are the block's weekend expert on cleaning and polishing automobiles. The neighbors admire your taste.

Then it happens.

A visible scratch, dent or fender bender takes that $40,000 and turns it into a $20,000 eye sore. The honeymoon is over.

Now what?

See the difference?

MEET THE CLICKERS

There used to be a time when you would be happy to see one of your images get published for free or you made $25 and had your name in print.

Today, it's big $1,000,000 moneymakers of done right per month.

And that's just one.

Here's how this one works. Create 30 inflammatory statements.

- In god we trust, everyone else must work for it. Click if you agree.
- With god in my life, my world is wonderful. Click if you agree.
- Jesus is my Savior. Click if you agree.
- Jesus warms my soul like a cup of hot chocolate does in the winter's day. Click if you agree.
- Without Jesus in my life, I am like a ship with no wind in my sail. Click if you agree.
- I am a sinner who found salvation in Jesus. Click if you agree.
- Spiritual love is knowing god. Click if you agree.
- Knowing god is my ticket to eternity. Click if you agree.
- Jesus died for my sins, so I could go to heaven. Click if you agree.
- My world would be cold and empty without Jesus in my heat. Click if you agree.

- Southern women do it best. Pass it on.
- California girls have the sexist legs in the world. Pass it on.
- Wild women are the sexist women alive. Pass it on.
- Girls in wrestling in mud are hot. Pass it on.
- Tattoos are hot on women. Pass it on.
- Is it me or are women hot wearing old west costumes? Pass it on.
- There's nothing wrong with dying of old age with a smile on your face. Pass it on.
- Black is the sexist color of tight clothing on a girl. Pass it on.
- Biker babes do it best. Pass it on.
- Big breasted women in a wet tee shirt contest are enough to give me a heart attack. Pass it on.
- I carry a gun because it makes me feel like a big man. Click if you disagree.
- Marijuana should be made illegal. Click if you disagree.
- Smoking should be completely banned. Click if you disagree.
- Women in the military who posed for Playboy should get a Dishonorable discharge. Click if you disagree.
- Everyone who comes to this country should not pay taxes. Click if you disagree.
- Indian companies should be allowed to diminish IT salaries by 6% every year. Click if you disagree.
- All consulting services should be allowed to not

pay for retirement funds. Click if you disagree.

- The president is making America great again. Click if you disagree.
- Poor people are just lazy. Click if you disagree.
- All student loans should have to pay 30% interest. Click if you disagree.

All of these are bad. But people click on these like a religion. What they don't realize is that behind the scenes, that click is worth a thousand pennies or $100.

How does that work?

Simple. What you think your agreeing too, passing it on or disagreeing to is one of thousands of ads that were clicked on at the same time.

This is exactly how BITCOIN works but without the issues of a crypto key and transaction ledger.

You generate revenue by selling clicks. And this begs, why are these people getting away with this?

Before the Internet, a small business venture became a very lucrative advertising medium. It was called the restaurant placemat ads.

The problem with it was – which led to its demise – the logical concern was that the mats usage count didn't equal the mats advertiser's visibility expectations. Just because 300 of them are used every day doesn't mean potential customers ever saw the ads.

Well this "click ifs" still needed to push a product or service to make this work. Well, if you look real closely on your home page on Facebook, on the far right are sections where enough "click ifs" succeed, a link drop is generated, and no one knows the difference. Besides, this also works for another reason.

It isn't just the click, it's the amount of time that ad is seen.

Meaning, you may be on your home page for hours. Point: and those targeted ads on your page are there because you clicked on one of Facebook's placemats.

Yahoo has a humdinger of something similar. And because it's specifically geared to attract your attention based on information being sold from Facebook and other social media you use to theme their enticing "click-mes."

Here's how it works. Let's say you wrote this:

One day down while visiting my brother, Paul, down in Landstuhl, my brother invited me to take a trip with him in a North American Rockwell Saber liner – a T-39. It's an Air Force private jet.

Automatically, I'm thinking I'm in the Army and I'm supposed tell my CO that a private jet was going to come to Kitzingen Army Airfield and pick me up. Yes, we had plenty enough runway. But trying to explain why an E-5 in the US Army was going to have an Air Force private jet pick him up sounded hard for even me to not start laughing.

It did. But the point here is I mentioned it.

The next day, I go over to Yahoo and one of these supposed editorials jammed packed with ads that get sandwiched between the content captures my attention:

THE MANY FACES OF AIR FORCE ONE

And to the right, was a North American Rockwell Saber liner

So, I went through all 21 pages and never once was

North American Rockwell Saber liner mentioned or used. I had become a victim of one of the biggest ad campaign scams on the Internet today.

In fact, anytime you see a sponsored above something that comes across as an ego enticement is a SCAM.

Here's 12 of their lead-ins:

- You would not believe what he or she looks like today
- You would be shocked at what he or she looks like today
- Most people born before 0000 can't answer these questions
- Bet you can answer these 21 questions
- Photos of the Wild, Wild West you wouldn't believe exist
- We were shocked at his or her net worth
- The women of (James Bond, Star Trek, Disney Mouseketeers, etc.) then and now
- You'll be shocked to see him or her now.
- A sad day for Hollywood with a picture of Sylvester Stallone.
- 10 shocking facts about...
- Actors who died too early.
- Popular 1980 actors and actresses who are working for a living today.

Almost none of these use the enticing image used to get you to click on the ad bomb you just clicked on. But the take away here is this, if the ads are paying 1 penny per minute for their visibility then you're looking at 3 cents per minute times 21 minutes or 63 cents for every sucker who dives into one of these. If just 1% of 1 billion visitors per day click on one of these things, it makes for 6,300,000 hits.

Multiply that times 365, you get: $2,299,500,000 Digest 2.3 billion for a while. While I'm sure Yahoo has their hand out on this – just a guess, $120,000 per day or $43,800,000 per year. A measly 2 percent rounded off.

But that's the tip of the iceberg. You see, these advertisers do tease well and once off Yahoo, well, it's a never ending enticing eye candy store loaded with enticing leads that could keep you busy for hours.

This is the big league. Could be part of your revenue stream someday. For now, I'm just showing through what I know. Now, it's time to get to work.

FOUR FREELANCE BUSINESS TOOLS YOU CAN'T WORK WITHOUT

Sooner or later, you're going wake up to the fact that freelance writing is a business. Hopefully sooner than later.

The following are six must have items that no business can afford to exclude.

BUSINESS LICENSE

While this may be optional, this is one item that could easily pay for itself over the course of a year.

When you register your business – fees do vary from state to state – you are, basically, applying for the right to be recognized as a small business owner.

What that means is you can go to a store, show them your ID and your purchase the what you need to run your business at wholesale prices.

Furthermore, many states have a tax on those same products sold to consumers. You don't have to pay that either.

BUSINESS CARD

Once you have your business name application in for a business license, the next step is to create a business card.

No business worthy of being called one doesn't use a business card. When used correctly, it does more for your business than you think. In fact, you may want to think of it as the handshake that keeps on shaking.

While that may seem to be a corny phrase, the fact is, your business card is also viewed as your silent partner.

Why?

Because a business cannot be remembered without some way of reminding a potential customer that you exist, and you are available for freelance work.

You may handshake your potential your potential, strike up a great conversation and there might just be a hint of potential work, but the business card is what will remind that customer of that first impression and make it easy for the customer to get in touch with you.

Also, business cards are often used by business stores and shops whose interest is in promoting their business and exchanging business cards between other businesses in town.

A business card is also important as an addition to a formal letter of introduction. Which brings us to exactly that topic

FORMAL BUSINESS TEMPLATE BASED FORMS

No one likes a formal template-based business letter sent to them unless that letter speaks directly to them about how, what you are offering is going to enhance their opportunities to make even more money than what they are making today.

Let's face it, unless you have 365 days free to travel about town, meet all the local business owners and take an hour of your time each day to talk with each one, a list of small businesses in a database and a standard introduction letter that fills in the name and the point of contact in the salutation and then send to each by fax, email or regular mail.

The funny thing about it is, while most people call this spamming, if you can really increase business for hundreds of potential customers, how else are you going to get the word out to them. And, there is another problem you must address right off the bat. "How much do you charge?

There are 2,080-man hours a year. $100 per hour is $208,000.

But it is not just the hourly fee you should consider charging for your work, if it is an enticing, attention getting promotional news release, for example, that kind of work should be based on a percentage of the profit realized by it and any other on-going profits made from the initial effort.

After all, if the company affected positively by your efforts stands to make $200\hour x 40 hours and 100 customers decide to purchase those hours, it makes sense that $80,000 should be going into your pocket.

The point here is, there is a multitude of ways you can make money; none deal with starting out giving discounts thinking you're having to break in. Standard rates and commissions is where you should start.

WORK AREA

You should have a work area where you work in solitude and without distractions from 9 to 5 every day. Yes, that means you're running a business. In fact, once you figure out that you can be running more than one business venture, the quicker you realize you can create a sizeable income and maintain it with the same effort as one.

Let's look at non-fiction. The categories are:

1. Reverse pyramid
2. News release
3. Hard news
4. Canned news
5. Business news
6. Art news
7. Group activity news
8. Lifestyle news
9. Military news
10. Business profiles
11. Regional news
12. Legal ledger news
13. Sports news
14. High tech news
15. State news
16. National news
17. Global news
18. Editorials
19. Obituaries
20. Calendar events
21. Photographs with cut lines
22. Human interest Features
23. Day in the life of
24. Photo features

And that concludes what I have to offer you as advice. From here on to the end reflect my trials and tribulations as a military Photojournalist. And believe me when I say this, every day was another in the life of a writer struggling against a Public Affairs system that was out of date, out of touch and in bad need of being restructure. How did I know this?

Department of Defense told me so just before I got out and told me I came close to doing it.

1973 WAS A GOOD YEAR FOR ME

I have this unique talent for being at the right place at the right time. So, before getting orders to head From Fort Huachuca, AZ, to Fort Campbell, KY, I would wind up taking an image of an Ordnance Officer standing on a 500-pound bomb.

I didn't take this image, but he was standing on one of these drinking some milk. I personally thought was hilarious. This was the result of a train with 12 cars filled with 500-pound bombs caught fire and decided to make the middle of the desert outside of Benson look like a B-52 Arc Light bombing run.

The reason why I was allowed out there in the first place was because I was working for the Fort Huachuca Emergency Operations Center (EOC) and I took images of the aftermath to be used for the after actions report for both the EOC and Explosive Ordnance Disposal (EOD).

The picture of the Officer drinking milk while standing on top of one of those 500-pound bombs got published in the Serra Vista Herald.

The other humorous story here is that 1 of the 500-pound bombs was found in Tucson inside a damaged four car and the press had a field day, "OMG! If it went off it would..." was pretty much their theme song. If you notice, there are no fuses in them. So, our local EOD people unceremoniously went up to Tucson, place the

500-pound bomb on a mattress in the back of a 3/4 ton, secured it and then took it to Fort Huachuca where they blew it up into non-existence.

BACK TO THE 101ST AIRBORNE DIVISION (Air Assault) I GO!

I arrived at Fort Campbell, KY, with my wife and it just so happened that now Major Craig Gies was there, and we got to talking about my disdain for the 2/17th Cavalry verses being assigned to the 4/77th.

As it turned out, Craig invited me over to his house and said there was nothing he could do about the assignment. I met an E-5 – don't remember his name – at Craig's place – who was also assigned to the 2/17th Cavalry and to the same Troop I was being assigned to.

After arriving, that E-5 came up to me and asked, "Did you really do the things he said you did?"

"Was it good or bad?"

The E-5 looked a bit frustrated, so I said, "If you are talking about the time where I found a pair of tail rotor bearings when they weren't any of them in Vietnam, yes.

If you're talking about the time I took over 2 of our sections to the 2/17th Cavalry and told a Major there that I had a Direct Order from the Divarty Commander to put them there, yes. And if you are talking about the time where I single-handedly, helped to completely rebuild our unit from a logistics perspective after it pretty much got wiped off the face of the earth from a massive rocket attack, yes."

"As for the rest of the stuff I did, I can neither confirm or deny such mischief. What I can say is every day was uniquely different and never dull around Craig."

I worked on a couple of AH-1G Cobras for a few months and decided to test the waters to see if the Squadron would be willing to place more emphasis on my writing and photography skills verses me being a Cobra Mechanic.

So, I talked to LTC Burnett R. Sanders. Sanders was not only interested, he was 101% percent behind what I was about to do.

When I knew him, LTC Burdett R. Sanders stood all 5'7". He was instrumental in developing a morale intensive environment for the 2nd Squadron, 17th Air Cavalry.

The first part of this environment included creating a program that brought the soldiers into the world of the mission tasking.

This was literally unheard of. Even in Vietnam, very few soldiers knew what was going on with respect to daily mission activities. Yes, the infantry was briefed on each task they were to perform but to have a similar daily briefing on mission activities which included all the soldiers involved simply didn't happen.

It did for each soldier involved with the 2/17 Cavalry between 1973 and 1975 when LTC was Burnett R. Sanders the commanding Officer.

The second part of this morale-intensive environment involved public affairs and more specifically me.

My job was to develop a program that would focus on the individual and how that job title played an important role in the success of that area of expertise and how it affected the overall performance of the Squadron.

Today, we call that process management. My job was to highlight all the sections that built up to Squadron level.

We accomplished this by providing Division Public Affairs with “Day in the life of” photo features, our “Out Front” newsletter, a very dynamically driven awards and decorations program and timely images – pictures without articles – to the editor of the Fort Campbell Courier.

When the 101st Airborne Division Air Assault celebrated its 101st birthday, it was my images that took up two pages in three different newspapers: The Clarksville Leaf Chronicle, The Courier Post and The Hopkinsville New Era.

Many of these images were of the Air Assault demonstration.

When we went to Fort McCoy, I was there to take pictures and to document – I was with the Blue Platoon when it launched an attack on the National Guard. I brought a screen and a move projector and showed movies.

When we went to Fort Bliss, TX, I went in a C-130 and took pictures of the C-5A as it opened the cargo door and we unloaded it.

When we went to Fort Polk, La, I went with LTC Sanders and, again, I brought a screen and a move projector and showed movies.

We weren’t just about Cobras and recon. We also had a ground Troop. D Troop used 106 recoilless rifles. Photographing them in action was awesome.

I remember, once, taking a picture of a jeep dropped at 500 feet from under a chopper. Wasn't pretty.

We didn't just photograph exercises.

When the women of the officer's wives club went to a retirement home up in Hopkinsville, I took pictures and wrote a story about it. I remember an older gentleman kept on insisting we see a young man at the retirement home. When I asked him what the age was of this young man, he said 53.

As I write this, I'm almost eight years older than that "young man"

We also once landed at a school up in Hopkinsville. I'm not sure why we did but one school teacher thought it might be nice if we could return with some of the other helicopters we used. So, we did after a few weeks and I took pictures and wrote the article.

There were times when we just had fun laughing at ourselves. Major McDermott comes to mind. I accidently took a picture of him holding the purses of then BG Jack V. Mackmull wife's gloves and purse. LTC Sander's wife thought that to be totally hilarious considering McDermott was well known for not liking to do such things.

So, I printed it up and it was given to Maj. McDermott during the hail and farewell ceremony for LTC Sanders. When Maj. McDermott wasn't happy at me he would billow out "Edwards."

This time I said while in the hallway, "I'm not here sir." That made everyone laugh.

As if that wasn't enough salt in the wound, then BG John N. Brandenburg asked McDermott to have me report to him, so he and I could have a picture taken together. Guess who had to take the picture?

It was sad to see such a good leader leave after a year and a half but that's the way of the Army. LTC Gary E. Luck assumed command.

Working interactively with the Division Public Affairs Office, I met John AG Klose and a Sergeant by the name of Charles "Chuck" Drake. Chuck was an extremely gifted and talented young man who was willing to work with me on my writing. With his help and with LTC Burnett R. Sanders approval and LTC John AG Klose's enthusiasm I managed to average a story and a picture in the *Fort Campbell Courier*. There were also times when 10 of my images were used over a two-page spread – known as a double truck – and published in more than one newspaper.

Not only did the military paper use the images, so did the *Clarksville Leaf Chronicle* and the *Hopkinsville New Era*.

In 1975, I re-enlisted and received orders to head to Germany. In January of 1976, I received a Commander Certificate and an Army Accommodation medal for the work I did.

But my work was just getting started. I still had a lot to learn about writing and photography. I just had to convince the CO and XO of the 3rd Combat Aviation Battalion (CAB), 3rd Infantry Division of that fact.

WHEN THINGS TO WORK OUT, RATCHET UP THE STAKES

I pretty much crashed and burned on my first attempt to gain traction on being the 3rd CAB. My wife arrived in Country and we had to leave to go back to the States because her brother died. I had an issue with my TA-50 gear being stolen back in the states and that didn't help. The camel's back got broken when the Inspector General (IG) Inspection found me to be in a critical job title.

No one wanted me but the Aid De Camp for the Harvey Barracks' 1 Star saw me on gate guard, wanted to know what I was doing there, and I told him.

One month later, I took over the Special Services Photo-lab. You can imagine what happened after that, I learned photography like my life depending on it. What I could do with film and photographic paper was amazing. Worked with color slide film and how to do Cibachrome.

About the same time, I was hearing about the 101st Airborne Division coming over on REFORGER 76. On top of that, my unit just had a change of command and the 3rd CAB was going to be sponsoring the 158th Aviation Battalion. Its Commanding Officer was LTC John AG Klose.

The local Special Services supervisor had added a new civilian to run the photo-lab, so I had plenty of time to take pictures of the soldiers from the 101st getting things ready for the rest of the 101st to arrive and I sent them back to the Fort Campbell Courier.

"NOT ONLY CAN'T YOU WRITE, BUT IF YOU COULD, OUR RIFTED OFFICER WITH A DEGREE IN WRITING COULD GET US PUBLISHED"

That's what the XO, Major Schley, said to me months back before I took over the photo-lab.

He threw me out of the library when I told him LTC John AG Klose was the Public Affairs Officer at the101st when I was there and is now the CO of the 158th Aviation Battalion whom which we were sponsoring during their stay in Germany.

When LTC John AG Klose did see me, he said, "Dick, what are you doing?"

I said, "Running a photo-lab, sir."

He said, "Not going to happen. Want me to talk to your boss?"

I thought, when does an E-5 have this kind of decision-making clout, but said, "Yes, sir."

"Okay, done. By the way, Public Affairs wants to know how you're getting images back to the states when no one else is doing it."

"I'm sending them through the Bundespost – the German post office."

"Have time to work with me?"

"Yes, sir!"

The 101st Airborne Division Air Assault conducts what's known as an Air Assault in Action demonstration. The Division was planning one for all the European dignitaries in Europe.

Up until recently, I couldn't prove that the images published in Army Aviation Digest were mine.

General John Wickham Jr was standing beside me when I took the image of the Huey under the camouflage and I gave him my camera, so he could see for himself how the image would look.

The humorous story here:

There are two.

LTC John AG Klose dropped me off where the Air

Assault in Action was to take place and I walked up to my enemy – anyone with a camera, I consider a professional rival – and asked, “Anyone know what is going on here?”

As soon as I asked the question, out in the middle of the field, “Dick Edwards get over here.”

Oh, geese, it’s my old boos, LTC Gary E. Luck. So, I went over to him started to salute him but instead he opted for a handshake.

“What are you doing out here?”

“Sir, I’m here to take pictures.”

Well, he got a bit testy, “I meant who gave you permission to be out here?”

“Oh, well, I’m running a photo-lab at Harvey Barracks in Kitzingen and my direct boss said it was okay. Also, LTC John AG Klose invited me.”

“Great, are you going to take some good pictures?”

“Yes, sir.”

“Where are you developing your images?”

I’m thinking, didn’t I just tell you?

“At my photo-lab at Harvey Barracks in Kitzingen.”

And I saluted him, he did the same and I walked away.

Now everyone wanted to know what I knew about what was about to happen. So, I told them. Got into position and got ready to take the pictures that you see above.

Second one:

So, I’m up in my lab and I’ve just finished processing the film and am running the prints through the dryer.

There is a knock on the door.

There is a second knock on the door.

There is a third and louder knock on the door.

I'm thinking whoever is knocking on that door can't read the closed sign.

So, I go to answer it and immediately stand at attention. It's a Full Bird Colonel.

"At ease. Are you Sergeant Edwards?"

"Yes, sir."

"I'm here to pick up pictures. Gary E. Luck sent me."

At this point, I'm beginning to wonder if there isn't something in the water or the European environment has caused the US Army to go completely nuts.

I get a LTC asking me if it is okay to talk to my boss and now, I have a Full Bird Colonel doing errand runs for an LTC.

Not only that, what would have happened if I decided to do the images later?

I have no idea whatever happened to those images past that point. What I do know is the 101st recommended an impact Army Accommodation medal but it was denied by the 3rd Infantry Division as I had just received one 8 months prior.

For those of you who don't know this, photographs seldom ever get used from unofficial resources. In fact, your job title is Journalist or photographer and the military pays for your film and your images.

Mine was AH-1G Cobra mechanic. So, me being neither, means I'm paying for the film and the prints.

I just knew it felt right to do what I did. As for the two units I worked with:

The Cobras of LTC Tom Denny's 4/77th Attack

Helicopter Battalion (Reinf) and LTC Gary Luck's 2/17th Air Cavalry Squadron accounted for 315 kills out of 464 aerial TOW engagements.

As for me, I was about to meet up with a man who would take what I didn't know how to do well and turn that into an asset. And that man was at the time LTC Gerald E. Lethcoe.

A few things I forgot to mention in the previous article, General Gary E. Luck is a retired 4 star.

Retired Col John AG Klose has passed away, and Chuck Drake who was instrumental in helping me with my writing is on Facebook.

The pictures I took that I'm showing which were published were only the tip of the iceberg. Apparently, the official photographers were not quite used to taking images of helicopters in the air and racing about with a bright sky causing their light meters to, basically, turn the helicopters into black silhouettes.

The head of USAEUR & 7th Army photographers and Video crews told me to send him all my negatives so that he could create a collection of images that he could send with press releases. I did, and he picked 12.

Getting slightly ahead of myself, then LTC Gerald E. Lethcoe was responsible for working with me on the REFORGER 76 images that were published in Army Aviation Digest that were shown in the previous article.

So, now that we're up to the point where the combination of all of what I had been able to do was about to be presented to LTC Gerald E. Lethcoe, only he was not seeing the past, he was hearing about me from then LTC John AG Klose.

I felt alone after REFORGER 76 came to an end

and the 101st Airborne Division went home. It was like I had to say good-bye once again to many people who shaped my life. And that to the fact that the Adrenalin rush you get having hundreds of choppers flying over your head at 100 miles per hour and when all that fades away and your left standing in front of a tall lanky dude who has the power to tell you your story ends here.

That's scary!

Let's continue into the world of the 3rd Combat Aviation Battalion (Provisional)

THE LEGACY CONTINUES

LTC John AG Klose told me, before he left, "You need to talk to your boss, I've talked to him. You need to talk to him.

Well, I finally got the nerve up to talk with him. He was down stairs in the wood working shop building a bid house. I told him who I was, what I was doing and why my passion for photo-features was more important to me than running a photo-lab.

He sized me up. I'm not exactly what you call skinny. In fact, I was right at the line where you start thinking about losing 10 pounds to say in the military. Snowball's chance in hell was my thoughts as he sized my up.

"Well, Dick, you don't have to if you don't want to, but we have a training exercise you can go out with us on."

And I was thinking, "WHAT IS WRONG WITH THESE PEOPLE?? Am I in the wrong Army? When did this Army decide that you – an E-5 – can make any of these kinds of decisions?"

Of course, I said I wanted to very enthusiastically. Then said I had some concerns.

"Sir, Major Schley doesn't like me much."

"I wouldn't worry about him." The way he said it made me feel secure and confident that he would be out of the picture.

"What's the other concern?"

I have a brother down at Ramstein Air Force Base who works in operations for the private jets they use to fly VIPs. We are from Norway and he's got a flight going to Oslo next week. I told him that I would like to go but."

"What's the date?"

"Wednesday of next week. We're going to be dropping off an Air Force 1 star and be back the same day."

"Done"

I like done.

Do you know the funny thing about this story is, everything was set up, I went down to operations and asked if they had an inbound Air Force Jet? The look on their faces was priceless.

I waited for an hour and one of the operations said rather incredulously, "Sergeant Edwards, we have an inbound T-39 inbound requesting that you meet them on the runway."

What was also funny about this is during REFORGER 78, I would be down in the same operation area asking if they had a German helicopter inbound to pick me up. The one below took me to the Fulda Gap.

This time, I was head for the Fulda Gap. Again, I'm getting ahead of myself.

Let's also get the various TOW Cobras we used out of the way. First, there was the Q Model Cobra.

By the way, if you see this picture on the Internet and there is a byline on it other than mine, here's another angle of the same helicopter.

Tube Launched, optically tracked, wire-guided TOW Cobra came in three versions. The Q model pictured above was barely able to carry 4 TOWs and sustain a hover.

The more powerful S Model could. But it still had the distinctive French curve canopy.

Engine exhaust was not being directed up towards the rotor blades.

The S Model modified was distinctive in that it now had the anti-glare canopy.

The production S Model was a fully built Cobra from the ground up and had a very distinctive control mechanism that protracted from the right of the helicopter.

By the time I left the Army in 1979, the Apache was just starting to show up in Europe.

Built down here in Mesa, AZ I had the chance to get up close and personal with one.

Of course, it always pays to have a Material Science Engineer for a daughter who works for Boeing

Am I really that old?

MISSION OF THE 3RD COMBAT AVIATION BATTALION

The mission of the 3rd Combat Aviation Battalion (CAB) was straightforward. Create a battalion level unit of Aviation tank killers. Consisting of three

Companies

The 235th Attack Helicopter Company came from the states and were located at Giebelstadt Army Airfield became B Company. They brought with them 20 TOW Cobras.

A sister unit, C Company, was in Schweinfurt, Germany.

A Company and Headquarters Company were located at Harvey Barracks in Kitzingen, Germany.

While I never kept exact count, I believe there were to be 20 TOW Cobras for each Attack helicopter company.

Keep in mind, we were the mold from which all Combat Aviation Battalions either residing in Germany or coming from the states on REFORGER exercises would be modeled after.

General George S. Blanchard was the driving force behind this concept.

The concept was to kill tanks and slow down an enemy advance long enough to replenish and beef up NATO assets in such was way that it would make the WARSAW Pact think twice about attacking West Germany.

NATO needed way reacting to a Russian invasion of Western Germany with their massive –40,000 armored tanks and vehicles positioned on the east side of the East\West German border. Intelligence gathering saw an assault through the Fulda Gap as the most ideal point of entry that could (and never did) drive directly into Western Germany and take over Frankfurt.

It was NATO verses the WARSAW Pact.

With a theoretical 12:1 kill ratio, 80 TOW Cobras could easily destroy 960. Unfortunately, for the enemy, the kill ratio wound up being an almost insane number of tanks and armored vehicles being destroyed even before even 1 TOW Cobra could be spotted close to 1 mile away from the kill zone.

But we had to get there first and we had to promote the concept that the Cobra was, indeed, a formidable platform from which TOW missiles could be fired. The end results the inhalation of enemy tanks and armored vehicles.

Okay, so the first encounter with my new boss, I thought, went rather well.

But I still had some issues to deal with. I had an XO who hated me, I was physically too close to the line where the US Army considered me overweight, and with respect to my writing skills I was still terrible.

For some reason, battalion level stringers wind up getting assigned to S-3 or operations. I think it was because there never was a real MOS or official job description. So, what generally happens is, unless you fight for every inch of your own turf, you wind up being the S-3 gofer.

I needed my first break.

To add to the passion to hit the ground running, the 3rd Infantry Division saw another Edwards from the same family – namely my father – who also happened to know a Captain during the Korean War by the name of Pat W. Crizer. The same General Pat W. Crizer who is now the 3rd Infantry Division Commanding Officer.

And yes, I did know the 3rd Infantry song by heart

by the time I was 10 years old. Including the stanza that was removed from the song that was deemed "politically incorrect."

So, the first thing on my list of things to do was what we call these days networking.

The 3rd Infantry Division had two publications: Frontline and Pillars and Posts. I needed to contact the Editor there, let him or her know who I was and then figure out how to get that foot into the door.

As it turned out, the E-6 in charge of Frontline was also that rifted Captain Major Shyly was telling me about. And by the way, that E-6 was one hell of a good writer. A fiction writer whose work would be published in *Army in Europe* also known as *EurArmy Magazine* in a three-part series.

Lucky for me, I had already contacted the editor of *Army in Europe Magazine*, John Michael Coleman as two images from my photo-lab had been picked for last page winners of a monthly contest. One from one of my photo-lab enthusiasts and the other from me.

I also contacted the editor of *Stars and Stripes* – which would be a contact I would use during REFORGER 77 and REFORGER 78.

Normally, by the way, the Public Information Officer is responsible for the battalion level news releases and any "in house publications" such as the battalion newsletter.

With that in mind, I also had to come up with ways to make every effort work. Create stories that could be standalone stories, photo-features or just images with what we call cut lines – a picture with a small one sentence blurb about the photograph and image credit.

Wrap all of this together and you have the appetizers of what I had on my plate. LTC Gerald E. Lethcoe had a couple of his own. Army Aviation Magazine was one of them.

As time will tell the rest of the story, working with Hillary Brown of ABC News and David Allan Burnett who was taking images for Time Magazine.

And since I only want to say this once, without LTC Gerald E. Lethcoe's interest and ever pressing drive for making the 3rd Combat Aviation Battalion an integral part of the combined Anti-armor force of Armor and lethal TOW Cobras to be reckoned with and the all-out efforts of John Michael Coleman to put up with me and my thirst for learning how to write, I wouldn't have become so visible.

I was told before I left the Army in 1979 by Department of Defense (DOD) that I came very close to completely revamping the Public Affairs program for DOD. I thought they were trying to impress me, so I would go back to Germany and do the same thing I did for another Combat Aviation Battalion located in Nuremberg.

I told them that unless LTC Gerald E. Lethcoe was the Commanding Officer of that unit, or General John M. Brandenburg was the commanding Officer of that division was there would be no way I could pull off what I did over the course of the past 3 years. I didn't want to push my luck. And that was the truth.

There is no way as an enlisted noncommissioned officer that I could have pulled off half of the things I pulled off if it hadn't been for LTC Gerald E. Lethcoe. It was a mutual, combined interest and effort.

The problem is, there also must be a mutual, combined interest and effort on the receiving side of this, too.

At Fort Campbell, KY, it was LTC John AG Klose who was just as eager to help me – and I might add – help himself to my services. I can remember him having me take images of General John M. Brandenburg receiving an award from General Sidney Berry because the official photographer who took the image could get the image to him on time to make the next day's newspaper.

Or the time when I went over to the airfield and took a picture of Secretary of Defense Harold Brown because, again, he wanted the image to be in the next day's issue of the Fort Campbell Courier.

Unfortunately, the picture of the Secretary of Defense picture from me never saw daylight in the Fort Campbell Courier because a GS-13 from the AV Department on post caught wind of what we were doing and told LTC Klose that if he published another unofficial image of mine when an official photographer was assigned to taking it, he would write up LTC Klose.

Well, today, the Army really does have a job description and an MOS for it. Here's the Army's job description:

- Public Affairs Specialist (46Q)
    - Enlisted
    - Officer
    - Active Duty
    - Army Reserve
    - Entry Level

- Overview

The Army public affairs specialist participates in and assists with the supervision and administration of Army public affairs programs primarily through news releases, newspaper articles, Web-based material and photographs for use in military and civilian news media.

JOB DUTIES

Research, prepare and disseminate news releases, articles, web-based material and photographs on Army personnel and activities

Gather information for military news programs and publications within your unit and around the Army

Develop ideas for news articles

Arrange and conduct interviews

Write news releases, feature articles and editorials

Conduct media training

Short of the Internet stuff, I guess they were telling me the truth after all.

EVERY TIME YOU GO TO ANOTHER UNIT,
IT'S LIKE TRYING TO PROVE
YOUR WORTHINESS ALL OVER AGAIN.

Especially, if you are a helicopter mechanic suddenly pushed into a highly visible job and on one has any idea what that is. You could be a spy for all they know. Especially, when you report directly to this guy:

And so, there I was, once again putting my neck in the noose and hoping the chair under my feet doesn't get kicked out from under me.

So, I go out on my first assignment and as soon as

I do, who do I see who's madder than a wet hen. The one and only Major Schley. Whom which forces me to stand at attention and salute him. He then walked away.

I spotted LTC Gerald E. Lethcoe coming in for a landing and sitting in the left seat of the Huey and once the Huey stabilized, I stood on the skid and he slid down the window. He then pointed to a button and as I looked down his finger tapped my nose and he laughed.

Okay, I love this guy; he has a wicked sense of humor.

"Sir, I don't think this is going to work?"

"Why?"

"Because of Major Schley."

"Dick, don't worry about him, he's gone."

And he was. I think we sent him down to Brigade as a signal officer.

Knowing I needed to work on my writing, I pushed pictures over to Frontline with cut lines.

LTC Gerald E. Lethcoe and I worked on this:

On his floor and in his office. Which brings me to another point. Why would an Officer from the 3rd Infantry Division want to put together a montage of images of the 101st Airborne Division?

The answer that comes quickly to my mind is that it was a political investment. It was a way to pave the way for additional images we would take and make public. We had the only images of the exercise that were publishable.

One thing was for certain, take me or LTC Gerald E. Lethcoe out of this equation and from this point on, publishable content about TOW Missile attack helicopters, combined arms efforts and the stories about the men and women who made all this happen would have turned out to be a blank page in the history of Army Aviation.

When we got to this point, I knew it was time to kick my writing skills up to the next level.

The interesting thing is, today, I have a spell checker. And, should I fowl on a grammar, Microsoft Word will alert me to my non-compliance.

Furthermore, today, with so much of my work depending on writing and with close to 5000 bylines, I think I've learned how to write.

That wasn't the case back in 1977. I needed help understanding prose and I needed to assure this effort would not go wasted on one hit wonders. I needed a solid template that would work for almost every article I would create.

So, I called up John Michael Coleman who was the editor for – at the time – *Army in Europe Magazine* and asked him if there would be any possibility that I could spend a week with him, so I could better understand what I needed to do to get published in his publication.

Army in Europe Magazine was renamed to *EurArmy Magazine* a few months later.

To my surprise, John Michael Coleman welcomed the idea.

So now, I must convince LTC Gerald E. Lethcoe that a week on orders to be temporarily located down in Heidelberg and working with John Michael Coleman was going to be a positive thing.

Well, up until Wednesday of that week, I watched John Michael Coleman shake his head left to right meaning I wasn't harmonizing with what he wanted. This was bad.

Then he pulled out a copy of an older publication and said, "Here's the format. You tell them what you are going to say, you say it and then tell them that you said it.

"Read this article and imagine how what you want to say would follow that format."

The story was 1500 words, it had a hook for an introduction, narrated through why what was said was important, then worked through some important facts and from there to the end of the piece, it was a story line walk through of narration, quotes and action that ended the article on a positive note.

I read the article in disbelief. In front of me was the template I was looking for. Staring at me with those black and white beady eyes.

You don't tell: "Today, despite bad weather, we were able to fire our TOW Missiles."

You share the same with emotions:

Here's what didn't work:

"Early morning saw a sole figure standing in front of mobile operations center. Generators screaming confusion, snow falling softly on and around him.

As the door opened, a transparent second of heat, the aroma of freshly brewed coffee mixed with pipe tobacco was felt by the guard as the officer handed him a cup of instant salvation.

"We're going to go hot today, sir. I can feel it in my bones."

"I certainly hope so. We've been here for almost a week without a break in the weather."

For the men and women of the 3rd Combat Aviation Battalion (Provisional), weather at Wildflicken in the dead of winter with three days of snow paints a mission impossible picture.

They were out to fire the Tube Launched, optically tracked and Wire Guided (TOW) Missiles down range using the AH-1Q Cobra as their firing platform.

What they were experiencing so far was a fog so thick you could cut it with a knife.

Want to guess what did?

The fog was so thick you could cut it with a knife.

Mixing some of the stuff above so that:

"We're going to go hot today, sir. I can feel it in my bones."

"I certainly hope so. We've been here for almost a week without a break in the weather."

Doesn't sound like cardboard cutouts you threw into the mix to make the drama about as drinkable as that cup of coffee.

Also, I'm doing a lot of paraphrasing as the first article accepted by John Michael Coleman was 40 years ago.

So, what is this template called? Faction. That's right, add fiction to facts and you get faction.

It isn't that you are telling the truth, you are. It is just embellished with drama to get the reader involved and keep him reading to the end.

I produced 6 more within a month and submitted them to him. John Michael Coleman called me and asked if I could come down to Heidelberg for a day next week.

I told LTC Gerald E. Lethcoe this and he approved the one-day travel. One of our own OH-58 helicopters flew me there and back.

"I'm not going to be here next month, so if you send me any more of these articles, don't expect me to answer."

"Okay."

"I want to take your Cobra Crew Chief article with me and submit it to Soldiers Magazine, if that's okay with you."

At this point, I was in a state of shock. *SOLDIERS MAGAZINE*!!!???

As far back as I can remember, the only people who got published in *Soldiers Magazine* were the best of the best.

"Are you sure it is something that they're going to be interested in?"

There was a smirk on his face like he and Soldiers Magazine were the best of buddies.

"It's good enough."

So, I wrote 6 more articles and submitted them to John Michael Coleman and waited.

On April 1st, I got a call from some Sergeant down at USAREUR and 7th Army congratulating me on getting my work accepted by Soldiers Magazine.

I figured it was a joke as he called me on April Fool's Day.

Turned out, it wasn't and was one of 5 that would get published from 1977 to 1979.

The second one accepted was called "Cotton Candy Carnival" and was a photo-feature and was also done while stationed in Germany and with LTC Gerald E. Lethcoe as my boss.

Another 6 more articles were sent to John Michael Coleman.

This went on from February 1977 to June 1977. By that time, John Michael Coleman had accepted 27 articles. And the 3rd Combat Aviation Battalion was seeing it's over the top share of publicity.

Well, all things must pass, and John Michael Coleman informed me that he would no longer be the editor for *EurArmy Magazine* and that a Caption Lynn Havok would be taking over his position.

I was told that all the stories he accepted would be used. They were. Lynn Havok called me and told me he was planning on using my articles but not two at a time anymore. So, I was reading my articles while I was back in the states in 1978.

WHEN A HELICOPTER HAS AN ACCIDENT HAPPENS, WHO ARE YOU GOING TO CALL?

That be me. It was one of those additional Add On jobs LTC Gerald E Lethcoe add to my plate.

There was a total of three helicopter accidents and 1 U-21 accidents that I was tasked to take pictures of. None were fatal and two were so humorous the way they happened that I'd like to go into some detail about them.

Let me get the least two interesting ones out of the way.

AH-1Q TOW Cobra

While returning from a training exercise, the group of helicopters experienced an almost white out condition due to an isolated snowstorm that they encountered. One of the AH-1Q TOW Cobras settled down on what the pilot thought was solid ground.

When the pilot in command rolled off the power to the blades, the helicopter rolled sharply to its left side, the blades hit the ground and were destroyed. The Cobra was a total loss.

The other incident involved an OH-58 when the pilot was flying using nap of the earth tactics came up to a high point in the terrain pulled pitch and flew right into a high-power line. While the blades stayed on the helicopter they were terribly damaged and the only thing keeping the entire transmission and rotor section was the bolt on the 5 mounts.

The first most memorable incident occurred while I was taking images for my Drowning Is Dumb article for *EurArmy Magazine.*

Apparently, two pilots – both CW4s – were doing touch and goes on our Harvey Barracks 8000-foot-long runway while flying a U-21 aircraft. One feathered one of the engines to stimulate an engine failure. The other elected to land the aircraft as the wheels began to retract. For 1900 feet – I know this because I had to take pictures where the tips of the propellers nicked the surface of the runway and counted the distance.

The plane eventually came to a stop in the grassy part of the runway, intact with more ego bruised than the aircraft itself. After I took the images around the aircraft and inside, the plane was moved to the outside of the hanger, the engines were removed and replaced, and the plane was flown from Harvey Barracks back to Heidelberg.

This one involved a friend of mine by the name of Captain Harry Patterson and it occurred down in Stuttgart during REFORGER 77. Apparently, Captain finally convinced our operations Master Sergeant that helicopters were safe to fly in.

Well, as it turned out, the fuel filter got clogged up and caused the engine to fail.

If you've been in Germany, you know that the streets in the small towns are very narrow. And Captain Paterson almost pulled off a beautiful Hail Mary landing. I say almost because there was a street light in the way. Upon hitting the pole, the main rotor blades removed themselves from the helicopter, hit the corner of home and ended up in the back yard of the owner's home.

Here's where it gets funny. Still dazed from the landing but safe – so was the Master Sergeant, I should add – Captain Patterson found himself in a bear hug from the owner of the home thanking him for not crashing into his home.

I still get a chuckle out of that. And we had to drive into town to take the images of the downed helicopter. Once the images were developed and in the right official hands, we were given permission to remove the helicopter from the street and that was the end of the incident.

They say that when one door closes, and another opens. Problem is, I always must hunt in the dark for that other door.

So, I looked up the *Time Magazine* Correspondent in Cologne, a guy by the name of Barrett Seaman, called him up and told him that if he would show up at the

Press Center the first Monday of the first week during the REFORGER exercise, I would get him into the front seat of a AH-1Q Cobra.

He got all enthusiastic and told me he was looking forward to it!

(Boy, was I talking through my butt!)

So, I went downstairs, knocked on my boss's door and heard LTC Lethcoe invite me in.

"Sir, is there any way we can possibly go to the Press Center on Monday the first week of the exercise?"

"Do you need to go over to the Press Center?"

"Not really. Barrett Seaman, the *Time Magazine* Correspondent up in Cologne, and I got to talking and he mentioned that he'd love to take a ride in one of our Cobras."

I was fully expecting the wrath of God. Instead, I got, "Wow, that's awesome! I'll do my best to make that happen!"

It was a more of a why didn't I think of that tone. And then, there was a time on April 27th when my wife went into labor and first daughter was on her way and he called me and told me he was trying to get me to Wurzburg from Heidelberg via OH-58.

I ended up riding in the back of a 5-ton truck and got there just after my first child was born.

But he did try, as the weather was nasty for flying that day.

Tuesday, we showed up at the Press Center and I was totally surprised at what I saw. It was a buzz with typewriters pounding out content, the place was two stories high, filled with a mix of tobacco products including pipes, cigars, cigarettes and writers and photographers none of whom I knew.

There was a bit of ruckus behind me and I turned around to see Hillary Brown of ABC News – she I recognized. I introduced myself and asked if I could be of service.

"I'm here to cover the WACS."

Well, we don't exactly call them that these days, I thought. "We have some working with us and I can get you a chopper in here tomorrow."

"Sounds great."

"Only one thing, we need you to cover our Cobras,"

"We're not here to cover the Cobras."

"Well, then, you can choose to take your chances and, perhaps, cover the WACS while they are out in the field training with us or you can get picked up tomorrow, do your story on the women in the field and cover the fact that it's the first time in the History of Army Aviation that a battalion of AH-1Q TOW Cobras assigned, trained and deployed in Germany has become the first of its kind formidable and lethal anti-tank weapons system."

"Pick us up a 9 a.m."

And we did. Not only did she get her story on the women in combat, but also our battalion was on TV the next night. Aviation tank killers were beginning to be accepted as a reality.

There was always the possibility of taking pictures. You would try to anticipate what was happening in front of your eyes and avoid being out of film at some key intersection of time and place. But sometimes the moment just wouldn't wait. Photojournalism — the pursuit of storytelling with a camera — is still a relatively young trade, but there are plenty of stories about those missed pictures.

In the summer of 1972, I was a 25-year-old photojournalist working in Vietnam, mostly for *Time* and *Life* magazines. As the United States began winding down its direct combat role and encouraging Vietnamese fighting units to take over the war, trying to find and tell the story presented enormous challenges. On June 8, a *New York Times* reporter and I were going to explore what was happening on Route 1, an hour out of Saigon. We visited a small village that had seen some overnight fighting but were told by locals that there was a bigger battle going on a few kilometers north. There, at the village of Trang Bang, I waited and watched with a dozen other journalists from a short distance as round after round of small arms and grenade fire signaled an ongoing firefight. I was changing film in one of my old Leica's, an amazing camera with a reputation for being infamously difficult to load. As I struggled, a Vietnamese air force fighter came in low and slow and dropped napalm on what its pilot thought were enemy positions. Moments later, as I was still fumbling with my camera, the journalists were riveted by faint images of people running through the smoke. AP photographer Nick Ut took off toward the villagers who were running in desperation from the fire.

In one moment, when Ut's Leica came up to his eye and he took a photograph of the badly burned children, he captured an image that would transcend politics and history and become emblematic of the horrors of war visited on the innocent. When a photograph is just right, it captures all those elements of time and emotion in an indelible way. Film and video treat every moment equally, yet those moments simply are not equal. Within minutes, the children had been hustled into Nick's car and were end route to a Saigon hospital. A couple of hours later, I found myself at the Associated Press darkroom, waiting to see what my own pictures looked like. Then, out from the darkroom stepped Nick Ut, holding a small, still-wet copy of his best picture: a 5-by-7 print of Kim Phuoc running with her brothers to escape the burning napalm. We were the first eyes to see that picture; it would be another full day before the rest of the world would see it on virtually every newspaper's Page 1.

When I reflect on that day, my clearest memory is the sight, out of the corner of my eye, of Nick and another reporter beginning their run toward the oncoming children. It took another 20 or 30 seconds for me to finish loading my stubborn Leica, and I then joined them. It was real life, unfolding at the pace of life. For some years afterward, I wondered what had happened to Kim Phuoc. She eventually left Vietnam for Cuba, and later, on a stopover in Canada, defected with her husband. They now live near Toronto, where she runs a foundation dedicated to helping children deal with the trauma of war. Nick Ut is still photographing for AP in Los Angeles. I think often of that day, and of the unlikelihood of a picture from such a relatively minor military operation becoming one of the most iconic pictures from the entire war — or any war. For those of us who carry our cameras along the sidewalk of history for a living, it is comforting to know that even in today's digitally overloaded world, a single photograph, whether our own or someone else's, can still tell a story that rises above language, locale and time itself. Except for one photo, which was published in Life the next week, my own pictures have lived in my archives for 40 years, like witnesses in waiting — until now.

"This is going to get interesting."

And it did. The Public Affairs Officer called in a Zulu time pickup. So, we landed at 9 a.m. instead of 8 a.m. Not only that, we were flying a Huey with a condition red X problem where because of the fuel indicator malfunctioning, we had to land every 25 minutes and top off the fuel tanks.

The second time we landed, Burnett lost it. Between all the yelling and dirt kicking, he made it clear as I also figured out that we needed to change choppers. So, this was explained to Burnett and luck switched sides.

I should explain at this point who I was sitting with. On the right side of the helicopter sat three photojournalists: me, Rudy Williams and David Allan Burnett.

The first photo-op had both Burnett and me in stitches. We were both cutting up so badly, the pilots looked back to try to figure out what was so funny. We also noticed that Rudy Williams did see what we saw as being so funny.

I went hot with the mike. "Sir, we need to land."

So, what was so funny? Picture two GIs sitting at a picnic table casually eating lunch behind them in a small open area were tanks and APCs with their guns pointed directly at them.

It was one of those, "What, me worry" moments that was a humorous image asking to be taken.

After eating and changing choppers, we got too busy to remember much about what we were taking images of. Just that the action shots were out in front of us and there was a lot to pick and choose from.

Suffice to say, some of the images I took in black and what were also taken by Burnett and published in *Time Magazine.*

There were three other times when I saw Burnett out in the field after that. Once when I was with my boss and we were watching the drop of an APC out of the back end of a C-130 and once again at the Press Center.

You can see the video of this here.

We arrived with the AV team that took this video. Because they had to set up rather quickly the tops of our choppers show up in the image.

There was supposed to be a 4th time but my boss stopped that. We had brought some of the press up to where General Alexander Haig had flown in by helicopter.

I was within a quarter mile of him but was stopped by my boss who told me that because I was overweight, I would not be able to go take pictures of General Alexander Haig.

Little did he or I know that this event stopped me from getting published in Newsweek who told me that had I had an image of a prominent figure, they would have published my work.

When I did say goodbye to Burnett at the press

center, I wanted to see if his ego was a big as his hair do.

So, I asked, "Do you think I have a chance getting published in Time or Life?"

To this day, what he said next, I will remember for the rest of my life:

"It is not a question of whether or not you have a shot at getting published in Time or Life. It is more a question of do you have the willingness to continually send them your best images until they use something you've made available to them. You must have your name on each slide and you must have cut lines for each image.

Never give up."

Bob "Silver Fox" Crossly, Director of AV at USAREUR & 7th Army told me to send my images to him because the images he had were bad.

"I'm going to need a ride over to Rammstein AFB, so I can use the photo-lab there. The guys developing the images at the Press Center are using a film developer that takes about 5 minutes to process film. And the results are horrifying.

"That will also keep me out of the hornets' nest for a day and I will have better control over my work."

"Done."

Again, I like done.

The next day, one of our S-2 Officers, a very mad West Point Officer flew me over to Rammstein AFB.

My brother met us on arrival.

"Who the heck is your brother?"

"I'm a West Point Officer and I had to fly your enlisted brother here from Stuttgart to Rammstein

AFB."

I looked at my stunned brother and smirked slightly, "Sir, I have between 3 to 4 hours of work to do at the photo-lab here. Don't know if you've been to Rammstein before but this is big base. Or if you want, you can leave and I'll lima line in to Colonel Lethcoe and tell him I've completed my work."

"Make it 3 and I'll wait."

"Yes, sir."

I pushed 10 rolls of Ilford Pan 100 using Microdol-X 3:1 at 72 degrees for 11 minutes. Within the first hour, I was done with the film processing and had one hour to work on prints, 30 minutes to work on drying them and 10 minutes to get back to the OH-58.

"Good, you're early."

"Want to see the prints, sir?"

"Sure."

He started going though all 50 of them.

"I want this one."

"Sir?"

"Can I have this one?"

"Yes, sir."

"These are really good," he said in amazement.

I think it was starting to sink in as to why it was so important to come to Rammstein.

Something was starting to change, and I wasn't quite sure why it felt wrong.

What I did know is what I didn't know was making me feel very close to falling off my high horse.

And I had already been warned by some senior non-commissioned officers that the meat grinder was waiting for me should that happen. I no longer had

John Michael Coleman. I was doing things way above my pay grade. I had to fill out my own award recommendation – singular, not plural.

And a had to put up with a performance assessment by LTC Gerald E. Lethcoe which, basically, spoke volumes about being thrown under the bus because, suddenly, it was much better to have done nothing and specialized on soldiering than it was to have significant impact through public affairs efforts on our unit's identity and awareness.

LTC Gerald E. Lethcoe had a few months to go on his 18-month cycle of job titles. It was like everyone was disappearing and I was left with a no promotion or advancement check.

I even had LTC Gerald E. Lethcoe's replacement call me up. How many enlisted men have their new Battalion CO call them up three months before they take over?

But the real clincher that convinced me it was time to move on?

When we took David Burnett over to take pictures of General Alexander Haig and LTC Gerald E. Lethcoe stopped me from going with him to take pictures of him.

Citing my being overweight as a public sore eye for the Army.

What LTC Gerald E. Lethcoe didn't know was I was also in contact with the editor of Newsweek and was told afterward that had I been able to have been able to take a picture of General Alexander Haig, they would have used my images.

Bottom line, it was time to move on.

But where?

NO LONGER A STRINGER

The Army made that decision for me.

As far as I can tell, this was also a first for the Army: a soldier, a 76Y20 Cobra Mechanic in a critical shortage MOS, was assigned on orders to the 101st Airborne Division Public Affairs Office directly from USAREUR and 7th Army.

So, considering what was just said about the job conditions at the 3rd CAB, there were certain people who saw the accomplishments and not the man as his true worth and potential.

LTC Gerald E. Lethcoe and I put this montage of images together and it was published in Army Aviation Magazine before. I left Europe I have no idea why the montage included the 101st Airborne patch as, clearly, the 3rd Infantry patch is on the shoulders of the soldiers photographed.

IN CONCLUSION

The worst was the best and the best was impossible for anyone to believe.

A battalion level stringer who paid for his one camera equipment, film and photographic papers. Out of his own pocket, worked with Hilary Brown, David Burnett, had 27 articles accepted by *EurArmy Magazine,* 2 by *Soldiers Magazine*, pictures published in *Frontline, Pillars and Posts, The Fort Campbell Courier, Army, Army Times, Army Aviation Digest, Army Aviation Magazine, AARES* (A Holland Publication), worked with Diana Dannis of AFN TV, the AV team from USAREUR and 7th Army and *Stars and Stripes*.

I was also asked to take images at the Army Aviation Association of America convention in 1978

All in 9 months.

Despite my dyslexia and my weight issues and my weaknesses in writing, I still managed to prove Major Shyly wrong. I did get my unit published but that wouldn't have happened without LTC Gerald E. Lethcoe and John Michael Coleman edging me on and honing my writing skills.

If there is one thing I've learned which holds true for every job I've had, is the fact that the job you had before prepares you for the one you're about to be part of. Regardless of its initial outcome, staying firm in your beliefs, hold purity in your heart, and striving to be the best at what you do trumps disappointment.

You can't make people like you. But you can always like them.

So, after I left the 3rd Combat Aviation Battalion, 3rd Infantry Division, I wrote on the average of 7 articles per week for around 6 weeks. I don't remember how many of them got published but I know a lot of them did.

After that, I was reassigned to the 2/17th Cavalry with the official reason being my Cobra crew chief MOS was in critical shortage. The real reason, Soldiers Magazine pissed off the Department of Information Services trained journalists off because they were calling me and not them.

But it really didn't matter why, in truth, it had to happen. As a matter of fact, everything had to happen.

I just didn't know why at the time. In fact, why is sometimes realized in bits and pieces.

So, in March, the first piece of the puzzle aligned. Major General John M. Brandenburg was about to become the Commanding Officer of the 101st Airborne Division. Yeah, the same General who requested a picture of me with him.

Believe me when I say this, when General Brandenburg came over to my unit to meet with my Commanding Officer, I tried to hide from him. Unfortunately, he spotted me, excused himself from the others, turned around and walked up to me.

I saluted him, and he saluted me.

"Sergeant Edwards, didn't I just send you to Germany?"

"Yes sir."

"What are you doing back?" He laughed and walked away.

Now, I knew why everyone was stir-fry nuts in Germany.

And, now, suddenly, my Commanding Officer at the 2/17th Cavalry found himself in a rather uncomfortable situation. He just witnessed an E-5 who was cozy with the Commanding Officer of the 101st Airborne Division.

Still, the exchange between us was hilarious.

You know, sometimes being bored out of your gourd is a good thing. And while I was waiting for REFORGER 78 to start taking shape, I thought about an issue that has been bugging me.

During REFORGER 78, the images were again mixed up:

At least, *Army Aviation* Magazine got the patch right this time.

Okay, so I was asked what was I doing back? Hum, well, I created a way to know what group in what troop had ordered manuals by putting extra holes in IBM 21 punch cards and that worked.

Up to that time, we had to call each troop to ask if they had ordered the manuals. After the inclusion, we no longer had to do that.

When REFORGER 78 was about to happen, I was assigned to A Troop, 2/17th Cavalry and asked to take pictures and write stories. I talked with and sent pictures to the editor of *Army Aviation Digest*, I had a black widow spider in my tent which was cool to watch the smaller spiders try entering my tent and then back out of it. Didn't know she was in there until I split my poncho apart from my half tent.

Apparently, she died as the flap of my poncho caught the chopper blades and pretty much smacked her around until she was dead.

Arrived in Germany with 20 rounds of 36 shots slide film, 6 rounds of 36 shots black and white film. For my semi-automatic 35mm packing a 28 mm lens and a sharpshooter 80mm to 210mm double barrel shot gun.

I was armed, and dangerous baby and I wasn't tank prisoners!

I know all the above sounded silly. But you must remember, I was back in country and the people I knew, the people who knew me were about to get a healthy dose Deja vu.

Sent Wertheim goes to Wertheim to *Stars and*

Stripes and then thanked the editor for publishing it. His last words to me, "Just like old times, Sergeant Edwards"

I swear on the stack of 500 bibles that I'm not making any of this up. So, I'm walking around all the evening activities, listening to the bitchy, high pitched screams of mobile generators, hearing the clanking of torque wrenches as rotor blades were being reattached to helicopters and I'm thinking, wow, I really have it made.

All I must do is get the pictures my CO wants and do what he has no idea what I can do here, and everyone is going to be happy. I'm back and, not only that, I'm back at Giebelstadt.

What could possibly go wrong in paradise?

You know what's coming, don't you?

I didn't.

I got back over to our GP medium and slept soundly until the smell of hot coffee and freshly cooked bacon drifted over my senses. After breakfast, we started throwing our gear into our duffel bags and preparing to go to the field.

Someone yelled "Ten-hut" and we all stood at attention. The voice from the colonel said, "At ease. Is there a Sergeant Edwards in here?"

"Yes, sir!"

"Report to General Brown, now."

How in the heck can a simple article published in *Stars and Stripes* be that wrong?

So, I reported to him.

"Sergeant Edwards, do you have film in that camera?"

MG John M. Brandenburg use to rib me with the same question. So, I wasn't sure how to answer him. I assumed he wasn't joking with me.

"Yes, sir."

"Consider that film and all the film in your possession to be official Army film. You are now the Task Force 229th official Army photographer."

"Any questions or concerns. No, sir. But I do have one concern. My CO purchased the slide film."

"You tell that Major that if he has any problems to report to me."

"Yes, sir. Thank you, sir."

I saluted and walked away.

I had no idea what just happened. I mean, wasn't I already doing this?

What now?

What has changed?

What was I supposed to do next?

And more importantly, how the heck am I going to explain to my CO that the film he bought just got compensated by the US Army?

So, I got back to the tent and the guys wanted to know what was going on.

"I don't think you're going to believe me if I told you. But here goes. So, the photographer who came over to take the official images for the 101st and for Task Force 229 got his leg broken while jamming it between a 5-ton and the trailer it was pushing back.

"I am now the official 229th Task Force photographer. Even I can't believe this is happening.

"Now, I have to tell our boss his film he bought for this is no longer his."

There was a good luck with that chuckle.

"He said w h a t!!!"

After the laughter died down. "Sir, I'm not making any of this up. General Brown told me to tell you that if you have any problem with this to see him."

"Alright, I'm not going to go see General Brown over the slide film and it looks to me like you're over your head, am I right?"

"Only on the logistics side of getting out to places and taking images of all of us here. The Task Force and not just A Troop, 2/17 Cavalry. As you have already seen with my Wertheim Goes to Wertheim piece in *Stars and Stripes*, I still have some ties with in country publications.

"The effort needs to include the Press Center for this exercise and getting the work back to our press folks from Public Affairs that are also here for this exercise."

"Forget the Press Center, let's keep your efforts in line with the chain of command expectations. Stay with us, I'll get you out to where you want to go and once a day, a chopper will pick up your work and get it over to our division Public Affairs staff."

"Thank you, sir."

I felt like Ernie Pyle. I would go out, take pictures and sit in front of my duffel bag while I typed on my portable typewriter. At 12 noon, a chopper would land, I gave them the film and the stories I wrote and never saw any of it after that.

On day three of the exercise, I went out with our Blue Platoon and took pictures of two of our soldiers riding speeding away on their motorcycles.

Notice that the 101st Airborne insignia is taped over. We were technically in enemy territory.

And I was loving every minute of it!

After dropping them off, we move to our pickup point. After we landed, it was obvious to me and everyone else on that chopper that we didn't exactly pick the best spot for a pickup point.

"Unless that's an earthquake, we got tanks around here somewhere. Sir, I'm going to look around the corner. See what's up the hill. If I give you the signal, we've got to go!"

I turned to corner and all I'm seeing is tank after tank after tank. So, I go up to the tank commander leading the first tank by foot. Snap some images and pull out my notepad and pencil and do what I generally do during a REFORGER exercise and start asking questions.

"Are you sure you're not the enemy."

"Yeah, I am and that's why I'm out here in the middle of nowhere taking pictures of you and your unit because I want to die trying to get my stories published in *EurArmy*. Do you read *EurArmy*?"

"Yes. Does Sergeant Richard Edwards ring a bell? Drowning is Dumb?"

"Wait a minute, you're that guy."

"No, I just stole the name just to come up here and harass you."

He laughed.

"Look, I have to go. Have a chopper to catch and get this back over to the Press Center. Thanks for making this article more interesting. Anything else you want to add?"

He shook his head.

I walk calmly back down the road, turn and when I'm out of sight of the tank commander, I give our crew the "let's get the hell out of there."

I buckled in, we raised to a high over to clear the trees, looked down, saw the referee who smiled at us, shook his head and gave of your dead for 30 minutes cut throat sign.

Oh, well, I tried.

Major General John N. Brandenburg once asked me what I was doing back after he sent me to Germany, the result of my efforts here during this REFORGER exercise was my way of answering that.

Major General John N. Brandenburg sent me a personal and official letter of appreciation after that and I was quickly reassigned to DISCOM in an E-7 slot, Public Affairs.

The last article I did for Soldiers was "Earning My Wings." It was about me going through the Air Assault School.

What was the funniest thing that happened before I got out?

Remember me being asked to take images of the AAAA Convention in Arlington, VA?

Neither did the 2/17th Cavalry. In fact, our Legal Beagle at the Cavalry called me a lie to my face when I told him about it. It troubled me, and I thought I had a pretty good excuse as to why I couldn't go when I got home from REFORGER and saw a note on the table:

Over at the hospital. Crystal is running a 104 temperature.

So, I called the AAAA Convention line, talked to a

colonel and told him to let Art know I have an emergency as my daughter was in the hospital with a 104-degree temperature.

Upon arrival back at Fort Campbell and since my Squadron Commander met me getting off the airplane and gave me the next 3 days off, I thought I was off the hook. Until Thursday night when a neighbor on the second floor told me that some Sergeant from the 2/17th Cavalry MUST talk to you.

It was our legal Beagle.

“Sergeant Edwards, why is the Secretary for General Kastner wanting to know why you aren’t on his airplane?”

Oh, did I want to laugh.

“Army Aviation Convention at Arlington, VA – ring a bell?”

“Never mind that, get the secretary off my back.”

So, I called Art, apologized. Told him what happened, told him the crisis was over and if they still needed me. I would be more than honored to go.

Orders were cut, and a Captain drove me to the Nashville airport in less than 4 hours.

At the end of the convention General George S. Blanchard told General Bernard Rogers to get out of his way because he wanted me to take a picture of him and an X POW Major.

General Rogers turned to me and said, “I don’t know, Sergeant Edwards, should I get out of the way.”

I’m usually lousy at standup quick response.

But I said, “I don’t know sir, which one of you has more time in service, time in grade? Pull rank.”

They both laughed and General Rogers got out of the way.

Publications with my bylines and credits from 1977 to 1979:

Air Force\Navy Safety Publication
Army Aviation Digest
Army Aviation Magazine
Army Magazine
Army Times
Army War College Review
Clarksville Leaf Chronicle
Lake Charles American Press
EurArmy Magazine
Fort Campbell Courier
Hopkinsville New Era
Soldiers Magazine
Stars and Stripes

Proudly served:

2nd Squadron, 17th Cavalry

Valorous Unit Award for THUA THIEN-QUANG TRI

Meritorious Unit Commendation (Army) for SOUTHWEST ASIA

Republic of Vietnam Cross of Gallantry with Palm for VIETNAM 1968

Republic of Vietnam Cross of Gallantry with Palm for VIETNAM 1968-1969

Republic of Vietnam Cross of Gallantry with Palm for VIETNAM 1969-1971

Republic of Vietnam Cross of Gallantry with Palm for VIETNAM 1971

Republic of Vietnam Civil Action Honor Medal, First Class for VIETNAM 1968-1970

Troop A additionally entitled to:

Presidential Unit Citation (Army) for DAK TO

Presidential Unit Citation (Army) for DONG AP BIA MOUNTAIN

Valorous Unit Award for TUY HOA

Valorous Unit Award for THUA THIEN PROVINCE

Meritorious Unit Commendation (Army) for VIETNAM 1965-1966

Republic of Vietnam Cross of Gallantry with Palm for VIETNAM 1966-1967

Generals I've known and talked to personally:

MG Sidney Bryan Berry August-73 – July-74

MG John A. Wickham, Jr. March-76 – March-78

MG John N. Brandenburg March-78 – June-80

MG Jack V. Mackmull June-80 – August-81

MG Charles W. Bagnal August-81 – August-83

MG Teddy G. Allen May-87 – August-89

General I knew before he became a 4 star:

General Gary E. Luck

In 1980, in August, SAGA Magazine published: Killer Copters Our Deadly Middle East Weapon.

For me there's never been a meet destiny half way. I spent ten years trying to make Cobras, their pilots and the people who support them look good.

I spent more than $10,000 dollars of my own personal income to do it.

The 4th Battalion, 77th Field Artillery was where this

got all started. I give me chill bumps to know the 229th was the 4th Battalion, 77th Field Artillery before it was renamed. I finished it.

Now that I'm retired, I look back and wonder if anyone remembers me or wants to make my golden years just as memorable.

Thank you for reading.

Please review this book. Reviews help others find Absolutely Amazing eBooks and inspire us to keep providing these marvelous tales.

If you would like to be put on our email list to receive updates on new releases, contests, and promotions, please go to AbsolutelyAmazingEbooks.com and sign up.

About the Author

Richard T. Edwards's life has been full of some pretty amazing people places and things. As a seasoned writer and photographer for the past 50 years he has had over 2,000 bylines.

The New Atlantian Library

NewAtlantianLibrary.com

or AbsolutelyAmazingeBooks.com

or AA-eBooks.com

www.ingramcontent.com/pod-product-compliance
Lightning Source LLC
Chambersburg PA
CBHW060306100426
42742CB00011B/1878

* 9 7 8 1 9 4 5 7 7 2 8 7 0 *